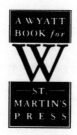

A WYATT BOOK *for*

ST. MARTIN'S PRESS

a wyatt book
for st. martin's press
new york

Guerrilla Cooking

The Survival Manual for People Who Don't Like to Cook or Don't Have Time to Cook.

Mel Walsh

Book Design by Gretchen Achilles

Library of Congress Cataloging-in-Publication Data

Walsh, Mel.
    Guerrilla cooking / by Mel Walsh.–1st ed.
      p.   cm.
    ISBN 0-312-14610-8
    1. Cookery.   I. Title.
   TX714.W262   1996
   641.5–dc20

                                 96-19101
                                 CIP

First edition: September 1996

10 9 8 7 6 5 4 3 2 1

**To my Queen Mother, Lucy II,
Matriarch and Patron Saint
of this Guerrilla Cook**

Table of Contents

Guerrilla Cooking

Introduction

What Is Guerrilla Cooking?

Fast-strike meals that are cheap, bold and fun—that's guerrilla cooking. And this cookbook is the field manual, your guide to waging unconventional warfare in the kitchen. The focus here is on timesaving maneuvers and quick-cook tactics, even if they are politically incorrect (cake mixes) or unorthodox (indoor picnics).

The recipes call for reasonably priced ingredients. No caviar in these pages. Also no running all over town for expensive, exotic materials. This is a mashed-potatoes-and-chicken kind of book—folk cooking, grass-roots cuisine.

Guerrilla Cooking starts where most of us need help: daily dinner. The first two chapters are full of recipes that will win the weekday battle against time and monotony. And monotony is a problem for the home cook. Most of us have ten dishes we know how to do—and that's it.

"What's for dinner, dear?"

"Number five."

So *Guerrilla Cooking* can help. Just think of it as 911 for dinner. Some of the recipes are so easy and fast, you can train your older kids or reluctant other to do them.

Next, the book presents super-fast appetizers and desserts for those times when you need to cook beginnings and endings but have menu amnesia about what might work well for your eating audience. If you are not at ease with cocktail tidbits or fluffy desserts, these chapters will boost your confidence.

Then, because we all need something we can cook really well, there's a chapter devoted to developing your own house specialities. Select your future forte from some twenty-five candidate recipes. You can learn to make popovers, easy chocolate cakes and fast mashed potatoes.

Last, since into each life some entertainment must fall, there's a chapter of menus and recipes to satisfy the people who show up at your door. And since all guests are not the same, there are ideas for picnics as well as down-home comfort meals, dinner parties and a cocktail buffet.

How Did the Recipes Get into the Book?

Simple.

They had to be simple. They had to be fast and good to eat. Most of the recipes have few ingredients, and those few are easy to find. As for reliability, the recipes were field-tested by real people who have no degrees in home economics. All recipes were cooked at least twice. Some, like the popover recipe, have been tested dozens of times. Over half the recipes invented were discarded as not quite good enough, too hard, too exotic, too too.

Much of the recipe development was a quest. How could I make a fast and lower-fat apple pie? (The one here takes twelve minutes in the oven.) How about quick chicken and dumplings? What was the best way to update good old macaroni and cheese? How could the dessert problem be solved without using heavy doses of butter and cream? (I lost 20 pounds working on this cookbook.)

Many of the recipes are low in fat. Some of the recipes use skim milk and nonfat cheese. What you do with these recipes in the privacy of your kitchen is, of course, up to you. Some people hate skim milk and may prefer to use the regular kind. Ditto for cheese choices.

We all seem to suit ourselves on the fat issue, depending on our age, concern for health, medical directives, personal preferences and, of course, what article we read recently. But if you have orders from your doctor to cut salt, fat, sugar or anything else, modify these recipes accordingly.

New Cooking Strategies, Plus Tips and a Place for Your Own Recipes

Because it pays to cook smart rather than long, *Guerrilla Cooking* doesn't stop at recipes, but presents strategies, smart ways to streamline dinner. You'll learn tactics such as avoiding cooking in the first place and minimizing one's lifetime exposure to food processors. One strategy is explained at the end of every chapter. Try these strategies. They work.

Also, because success in cooking comes from knowing the little things that cookbooks don't usually tell you, there are tips throughout the book, ideas and techniques for saving time and sanity.

At the end of the book, you'll find a short section called "Guerrilla Recipes from Home." These blank pages are the place to record your own guerrilla inventions. If you wish, you can pass them on to me at my guerrilla kitchen (gcooking@aoL.com) or at P.O. Box 2521, Aptos, CA 95001.

Spatter This Book

Last, an unusual request: Please spatter this book.

Cookbooks are like teddy bears—the ones that are loved are the ones that are tattered. If, over time, your copy of *Guerrilla Cooking* is covered with spots and flour fingerprints, you'll know you've found a realistic, user-friendly book that fits into your life.

Here's to good meals, more fun, many spatters.

—**Mel Walsh**

1 Daily Dinner:
How to Handle Weekday Desperation

THE DINNER DILEMMA

The Dinner Dilemma

There you are, facing the cooktop, knowing that the family and you cannot live through one more frozen pepperoni pizza. You must produce a real dinner. As they say in show business, you are ON.

If you are like the rest of us, you will not take the time to futz over complex recipes with sixteen ingredients and various choppings, parings and skinnings. Like a good guerrilla cook, you will refuse to peel tomatoes, burn the skin off peppers or carve mushroom caps. You just want to get a decent dinner out of the starting gate fast.

But one big barrier to getting dinner on the table may be the recipe itself. Isn't that ironic? Recipes and cookbooks are capable of telling lies. They claim they are fast, quick-cook or instant. Try them and an hour later, still hungry, you realize you've been had.

To defend yourself in the future, evaluate a recipe by counting the number of ingredients. If it's over eight, maybe you should move on. If the count is lower, bingo.

The following main-course recipes are fast. They begin where most family cooks begin; with pasta. They then move to another popular offering—birds, specifically chicken, with a few wing flaps from a turkey. The chapter ends with fish. We don't eat enough of them, but these few seafood recipes may change your mind or at least get the family to stop complaining about the fish when you *do* serve it.

Pasta

Get yourself off to a fast start with pasta dinners by setting the pot to boil (covered) before you open the mail or take off your shoes.

Angel-Hair Pasta Pie

Pasta pie makes cameo appearances on the family cooking circuit, but it is usually made with boiled spaghetti. This step-saving and innovative dish is made with unboiled (but baked) *fresh* angel-hair pasta. The kids will love this one.

1/4 cup water	8 ounces ground round
1 egg white	1/2 cup chopped onion
4 ounces fresh angel-hair pasta (from the dairy case)	3/4 cup store-bought spaghetti sauce
1/3 cup grated Parmesan cheese	1/2 cup shredded part-skim mozzarella cheese

Heat the oven to 350°. Oil or coat a 9" pie pan with nonstick spray.

In a bowl, combine water and egg white. Stir in the uncooked pasta and the Parmesan cheese. (Note that you are using fresh pasta, not the dry product. Also note that you are using only 4 ounces of the fresh pasta—about half the typical package.)

Arrange the pasta on the bottom of the pie plate, bringing it slightly up the sides but not up to the very top. The best part of the pasta lies underneath the sauce, so you want just an edge peeking over the meat sauce as a "crust."

Put the pie plate aside. In a large frying pan, cook the meat and onion on high until the meat is brown and the onion soft—about 5 minutes. Drain off the fat. Add the spaghetti sauce and mix with the meat and onion in the pan. Put the meat-spaghetti sauce over the pasta crust.

Bake uncovered for 20 minutes. Add the mozzarella and bake another 5 minutes. Let stand 5 minutes. Cut into four wedges and serve with a salad.

Serves 4 theoretically, as imagined by a registered dietitian, but a real-life quartet with large appetites could easily polish off two pies. Consider doubling the recipe.

Pasta and Baby Meat Loaves

This dish is a cross between spaghetti with meatballs and meat loaf. On the plate, it looks like little meat squares perched jauntily on a bed of pasta. A crossbreed, this recipe has none of the disadvantages of the parent dishes. (Meat loaf takes an hour to cook—a long time when the family is hungry. Meatballs are labor intensive—all that rolling and frying.) So here's a new way to produce a protein topper for your pasta without becoming a slave to dinner.

1 pound spaghetti (or your favorite pasta)
1 pound ground round
1 egg, slightly beaten
1/2 cup seasoned dry bread crumbs
1/4 cup milk

1 small onion, diced
1/2 teaspoon salt
1/4 teaspoon cayenne pepper
1 teaspoon Italian seasoning (a dried-herb mixture)

Set the pasta pot to boil. Cook the pasta according to package directions.

Heat the oven to 425°. Mix the remaining ingredients in a large bowl. Place this meat mixture on an ungreased baking sheet or pan with low sides. Pat it into a 6", flat-topped square in the middle of the pan.

Now cut the meat into 12 little squares, but don't separate them. Just cut all the way through the mixture with a knife and let the scored mini-squares huddle shoulder to shoulder.

Bake for 20 minutes, or until the meat is no longer pink in the center. When done, cut the mini-squares apart.

Serve on a bed of spaghetti. Spaghetti has been off the fashionable pasta menu so long, your family will probably think it's a new discovery.

This recipe is flavorful, so it doesn't need a sauce, but you can always add a favorite store-bought marinara.

A salad and a loaf of French bread will round out the dinner.

For an even faster meal, use a seasoned fresh meat-loaf mix. Meat-loaf mix often sits next to the ground beef in the meat case.

Serves 4.

Mexican Spaghetti

Use this one on the nights when you're tired and don't want guff from anyone about the menu. They all should like this, and if they don't, tell them it's their turn to cook tomorrow night. If you always keep a pound of ground round in the freezer, you can defrost it in the microwave and use this as your basic emergency meal. Except for the onion, the other ingredients will keep in the cupboard.

1 pound spaghetti
1 pound ground round
1 small onion, chopped
11-ounce can Mexican-style corn
1 cup chopped ripe tomatoes, either fresh or canned

2 tablespoons chili powder

Optional Garnish
Monterey Jack cheese, shredded

Put the pasta pot on to boil. Meanwhile, brown the beef and chopped onion in a frying pan over medium-high heat. Stir so they won't stick. Drain off any fat. Then add the corn, drained tomatoes and chili powder. Stir. Simmer with the cover on so the juices don't evaporate.

When the pasta is cooked, drain and put it into a serving dish. Pour the meat sauce over the pasta. If desired, sprinkle with grated Monterey Jack cheese.

Serve with a green salad topped by avocado slices.

Serves 4.

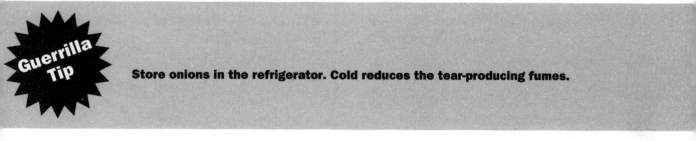

Guerrilla Tip

Store onions in the refrigerator. Cold reduces the tear-producing fumes.

A Macaroni-and-Cheese Renovation

While researching this book, I found that families still love that old favorite, macaroni and cheese. Many cook it from a boxed mix, but this recipe brightens up that same old taste. I experimented with several new versions of macaroni and cheese and this one was the winner.

The taste is subtle and rich on the tongue, an effect that comes from the use of smoked cheddar cheese. The nutmeg adds another dimension. Faster than many traditional recipes, this version does not call for oven baking.

1/2 **pound elbow macaroni**	3/4 **cup grated smoked cheddar cheese**
2 **tablespoons butter**	**Salt and pepper to taste**
2 **tablespoons flour**	1/8 **teaspoon nutmeg**
1 **cup milk**	

Add the macaroni to a large pot of boiling, salted water. Cook about 7 minutes. Drain in a strainer.

Meanwhile, melt the butter over low heat, using a heavy frying pan big enough to hold all the pasta and cheese. Stir in the flour. (Wondra, the instant-mix flour that comes in a round blue shaker can, is useful. I've never had a sauce or gravy lump up on me when using this kind of flour.)

Cook and stir for 2 more minutes. Blend the milk in slowly. Turn up the heat to medium. Keep stirring and bring to a boil.

As soon as the milk bubbles, turn the heat to low and stir 2 more minutes. Then mix in the grated cheese until melted. Add the macaroni, coating it with the sauce. Touch up with salt and pepper. A shake of nutmeg adds another subtle note.

If you want the crust of oven-baked macaroni, at this point, place the pan of pasta to brown under a hot broiler while watching the process through the open oven door. Make sure the handle of the frying pan is flameproof if you're going to finish the dish in the broiler. However, this recipe is fine without the bother and risk of broiling.

Best served right away. A green salad and a side of sliced ripe tomatoes would make a nice meal.

Serves 4.

No-Brainer 3-P Pasta

This dish is easy to remember without the recipe in front of you. When you're in the supermarket at 5:30 with no grocery list and no idea of what to have for dinner—a typical case of menu amnesia—just think of three ingredients that begin with the letter "P": pasta, peppers and pesto.

The pasta recommended here is radiatore—(rah-dee-a-TOR-ay)—a ruffled number with crinkles that hold the sauce. This particular shape delivers a lot of sauce to the waiting mouth, but use whatever pasta you like.

1 pound radiatore (or your favorite pasta)

3 bell peppers (try different colors: red, green, yellow)

1 onion

2 tablespoons olive oil

1 cup pesto (in little tubs in the deli case)

Grated Parmesan or Romano cheese

Garnish

Thin strips of fresh pepper

Haul out the pasta pot, get the water boiling and throw in the contents of the package. Cook according to package directions.

Meanwhile, back at the cutting board, slice the peppers and onion. (Reserve a few slices of pepper as a garnish.) Place the peppers and onions in a skillet with the oil (or in a nonstick skillet with no oil) and cook over high heat for about 3 minutes, stirring now and then. Turn down the heat and let simmer while the rest of the meal cooks.

As the pasta boils and the veggies simmer, attend to the minimalist sauce. Dump the pesto in a microwavable serving dish, one in which you can serve the pasta. (A high-sided soufflé dish will do nicely.) Microwave the pesto in the serving dish for one minute. (Or warm it on the stovetop, if you prefer.)

Drain the pasta. Dump the pasta into the warm pesto. Mix gently. Stick the simmered and beautifully colored pepper-and-onion mixture on top and serve.

Garnish with the reserved pepper strips.

Add grated cheese at will. A salad and bread sticks make this a meal.

Serves 4–6.

Save-Your-Bacon Linguine

This dish is a savior and can be on the table in minutes. It features just a touch of the lower-fat bacon—Canadian bacon—as well as a sprinkling of peas for color and comfort. Each serving has just one round of bacon and one-half ounce of cheese, so eaters can catch the flavor without eating mega-grams of fat.

1 pound linguine	**2 cups frozen peas**
4 slices Canadian bacon, diced	**Salt and pepper to taste**
2 ounces blue cheese (or shredded Monterey Jack cheese)	

Get out the pasta pot, fill with water and set it boiling. Cook the linguine according to the manufacturer's directions. Pasta is done when it is like a good mother: tender but firm.

As the pasta cooks, dice the bacon and crumble the cheese. In a large frying pan, preferably nonstick, warm the diced bacon over medium-low heat, stirring so it won't burn. Add the peas and cook just a few minutes until they are heated through but still bright green. *(Continued)*

Drain the pasta well and turn it into a large serving bowl. Add the bacon, peas and cheese. Add ground pepper as well as salt if you really need more salt. (Cheese and bacon usually provide plenty.)

A simple salad topped with chilled canned mandarin oranges and a loaf of herb bread will round out the dinner.

Serves 4 starving people who have not eaten too many snacks before dinner.

Seashells

Giant pasta shells are a meal for the whole household. Women of delicate taste enjoy this pasta because it's not rough fare such as a slab of steak. Men prefer the large shells because they are heftier than sissy stuff like angel-hair pasta. Kids can pretend that they are mermaids and mermen eating seashells; but if kids are in the eating audience, you may want to leave the capers out of the recipe or serve them on the side.

You may like this recipe because you don't have to go to the store. Just blanket the pasta with goodies already in your pantry or refrigerator and you won't have to turn a car key. Somehow, this recipe manages to taste fresh even though its origins are not so pure.

1 pound large pasta shells
2 tablespoons capers
6-ounce can water-packed tuna, drained
2¹/₄-ounce can chopped black olives, drained

2-ounce jar chopped pimentos, drained
1 teaspoon Italian seasoning
Salt and pepper to taste

Get a big pot of water boiling and throw in the shells. Stir now and then to make sure the shells don't stick to the bottom. (Like the real seashells they imitate, pasta shells like to hang out at the bottom of the water.) By the time the pasta is done—8 to 10 minutes—the rest will be ready.
(Continued)

The rest: In a pot, gently mix the capers, tuna, olives, pimentos and seasonings. Heat over medium-low until warm. Drain the pasta. No need to rinse. Pour the tuna mix over the pasta.

If you have fresh herbs on hand, add them. This dish is good with fresh oregano and lemon thyme. If you use fresh herbs, take the leaves off the coarse stems and chop the leaves to release the flavor. A tablespoon of freshly chopped herbs will do it.

Salad topped with thinly sliced red onions and cooked green beans plus a loaf of bread would round out this meal. A bit of grated Monterey Jack cheese on the pasta should not be refused.

Serves 4.

One-Pot Broccoli Fettucine

While writing this book, I got requests to find fast and good ways to get vegetables into the family. This recipe uses the pasta pot to cook the broccoli along with the pasta. As a variation, you could use cauliflower, which would look nice on a bed of green spinach pasta.

People who like broccoli will be happy with the recipe just as it is: olive oil, herbs, salt, pepper and grated cheese. People who aren't so sure will want to hide the broccoli under a thick sauce. Use one of the quick sauces below or your favorite store-bought pasta sauce—whether tomato, pesto or low-fat Alfredo.

Another choice: Coat the filled serving dish with a layer of sliced cheese and place in a hot oven (400°) for a few minutes until melted.

1 pound fettucine	**2 teaspoons Italian seasoning**
1 pound broccoli florets	**1 cup grated Parmesan cheese**
4 teaspoons olive oil	**Salt and pepper**

Put a large pot of water on to boil. When it comes to a boil, add the fettucine. Set a timer for 3 minutes shy of package directions: If the package directions say 10 minutes, set the timer for 7 minutes. When the timer rings, throw in the broccoli florets and let them bubble along with the pasta.

When the pasta is done, drain the pot's contents and place in a large serving bowl. Add the olive oil and Italian herbs and mix gently. Add grated cheese, salt and pepper as desired.

Serves 4.

Cooking two things in one boiling pot is smart because it saves pot-tending and dishwashing time. Adapt this technique to any vegetable that you might like to sling over pasta, whether sweet peppers, peas or mixed vegetables. Then just add seasoning, herbs, olive oil, sauces and/or cheese at will.

If you want to make pasta sauces from scratch, here are two fast recipes:

Fast Mozzarella Sauce

I invented this when I wondered why nobody seemed to use the favorite pizza topper, mozzarella cheese, in a smooth melted sauce for pasta. This sauce, made with skim milk and nonfat shredded cheese, is mindful of fat levels though it has a butter base. The recipe is good and fast.

3 tablespoons butter
1/4 cup flour
2 1/2 cups skim milk
1/3 cup grated nonfat mozzarella cheese

1/8 teaspoon ground nutmeg
Salt to taste

In a heavy saucepan, melt the butter and whisk in the flour. Cook over medium heat. Whisk constantly about 1 minute. Then pour in the milk. Stir and heat to the boiling point. Turn down the heat and stir until thick, about 1 or 2 minutes. Add the cheese and turn the heat even lower, again stirring. When melted, get the sauce off the heat so it won't burn. To keep the sauce warm, you can put a metal heat-diffusing round under the pot and turn the heat as low as you can without its shutting off. (Heat-diffusing rounds may be found in kitchenware shops and catalogs.)

Serves 4.

Quick Gorgonzola Sauce

This can be made with Gorgonzola or blue cheese. Both cheeses typically come in 4-ounce packages. The recipe calls for 3 ounces of cheese. Save the other ounce for crumbling on top of the pasta and sauce. Toasted walnuts scattered over the pasta would make dinner quite a dashing event. This sauce will suit many pastas, except, ironically, the nationally distributed fresh ravioli that's made with Gorgonzola and walnuts. Same on same makes a dull meal.

3 tablespoons butter
1/4 cup flour
2 1/4 cups skim milk

3 ounces Gorgonzola or blue cheese, crumbled
1/4 teaspoon pepper

In a heavy saucepan, melt the butter and then whisk in the flour. Cook over medium heat for 1 minute, stirring all the time. Whisk in the milk. Heat to the boiling point, stirring. Turn down the heat a little and stir until thick, about 1 or 2 minutes. Add the cheese. Turn to very low. Stir until melted. Remove from heat before it burns. Can be kept warm on low over a metal heat-diffusing round.

Fast Ginger Chicken

At last! Here is your chance to be a fine Chinese chef without a lot of chopping. This is a super-quick, easy way to prepare chicken breasts. It tastes as if you've taken the family out for good Chinese food. A top-of-the-stove number, this dish made with fresh ginger is both sweet and spicy. You can cook the basic version as in the recipe, or fancy it up as outlined below. If you have fresh ginger left over, stash it in a zip-top bag and store it in the freezer for the next time you make Ginger Chicken.

This is the dish to serve to people who think you can't cook.

4 boneless chicken breasts, total weight about 1½ pounds

½ cup flour

1 tablespoon cooking oil

½ cup orange juice

2 tablespoons honey

2 tablespoons soy sauce

1 tablespoon grated fresh ginger

2 garlic cloves, minced

Optional Garnish

1 tablespoon toasted sesame seeds

Cut or pull the skin off the chicken breasts and discard. (Scissors are an easy way to remove poultry skin.) Cut the breasts into slices. Place the slices in a plastic bag with the flour and shake until the chicken is covered. In a large nonstick skillet, heat the oil. Shake the extra flour off the chicken as you take it out of the bag.

Add the chicken to the hot oil. Brown the chicken about 2 minutes on high. Stir so it won't burn. Then turn the heat to medium high/medium and cook about 6 more minutes, stirring occasionally.

As the chicken cooks, mix the orange juice, honey, soy sauce, ginger and garlic together. You can warm this mixture in a glass measuring cup for 30 seconds in the microwave so the honey will mix more easily with the other ingredients. Then pour this sauce over the chicken in the pan. Bring to a boil. Simmer 3 minutes on low heat, or until the chicken has no pink in the center. Add a bit of orange juice if the sauce becomes too thick. Stir to get up all the nice brown bits of flour in the pan.

If you want a sesame-seed topper, toast the seeds for 2 minutes in the microwave or until brown.

This dish is great on its own, but it's hard to leave alone. Try adding toasted walnut bits with small pieces of sautéed sweet red pepper.

Another variation, this one Hawaiian: Add bits of pineapple and top with toasted coconut.

Ginger Chicken is good with rice as a side dish.

Serves 4.

Crispy Critter Chicken

This recipe is a way to sneak in the taste of forbidden food—home-fried chicken—without pan-frying the bird in a bucket of oil. It is a favorite of my test cooks. It is also the easiest and crispiest chicken around, sporting a crust made of potatoes, of all things—a crust that is not only decorative and crunchy, but acts as insulation to keep the chicken juices in the chicken.

Don't be thrown by the dehydrated potato flakes. Instant spuds have improved vastly over the years, and you don't have the time to wash, peel, cook and mash your own right now, do you? So the heck with from-scratch cooking, at least for tonight.

1 tablespoon cooking oil (or butter)
1¼ cups instant dry mashed potato flakes
½ cup grated Parmesan cheese

½ teaspoon salt
½ teaspoon pepper
2–3 pounds chicken pieces
2 eggs

Heat the oven to 425°. Coat the bottom and sides of a 13" x 9" rectangular baking pan with the cooking oil. Use a paper towel to swab the oil around. Easier still: a nonstick spray.

(Continued)

The idea here is to dip the chicken in beaten eggs and then roll it in a crust, so first beat the two eggs in a bowl. Then, in another dish, mix the potatoes, cheese, salt and pepper.

Now dip the chicken pieces in the beaten eggs and then turn them over and over in the flaky potato mixture until all the skin is covered with a snowy crust. Bake uncovered 50 minutes, or until done. Best served hot and crispy.

Add French bread and a green salad with ripe tomato chunks. Steamed or microwaved carrots would be nice.

To dress this dish up for guests, sprinkle with chopped macadamia nuts during the last 10 minutes of baking. When serving, garnish with a few more chopped nuts and some parsley. Serve a green salad topped with papaya bits and kiwi slices.

Serves 4.

Hit-and-Run Chicken

I invented this dish one suppertime when I wanted to sit with my feet up in front of the fire and talk to one of my sons. What could I cook that required just a few minutes of preparation? The guerrilla answer was this:

1 chicken, cut into pieces
6-ounce jar marinated artichoke hearts (packed in oil)
1/4 to 1/2 cup pine nuts

1/2 teaspoon dried rosemary (or a few sprigs fresh rosemary)

Simply dump the artichoke hearts, oil and all, into a pretty baking dish. Dieters can hold back on the oil and use just enough to coat the baking pan. Then add the chicken pieces, turning to coat them in the oil. Scatter the pine nuts and rosemary over the chicken. Bake one hour at 400°. Sit and relax with a family member.

Garnish with sprigs of rosemary. Good with potatoes that have been baked for an hour right along with the chicken. Buttered carrots can add color on the side.

Serves 3–4.

Guerrilla Chicken and Dumplings

Chicken and dumplings in every pot—that's my motto. But we today are chicken-and-dumpling-deprived. People don't make this dish because they assume it is a big deal. In fact, it is a super-snap dinner when you use shortcuts.

The "dumplings" are, in fact, baked refrigerated bread-stick dough placed on top of the bubbling stew at serving time. (In the store, this product sits right next to the tubes of buttermilk biscuits.)

Chicken Stew

2 14^1/$_2$-ounce cans chicken broth

1 package (1 pound) frozen mixed stew vegetables

1 pound skinless, boneless chicken breast, cut into small pieces

2 teaspoons *fines herbes* mixture (found in the spice section)

^{1}/$_4$ teaspoon pepper

^{1}/$_3$ cup flour

^{1}/$_2$ cup milk

Topping

10-ounce package refrigerated bread-stick dough

Heat the oven to the temperature suggested on the tube of refrigerated bread-stick dough.

Haul out a big frying pan. Dump in the broth and vegetables, bringing them to a boil. Cut the chicken into bite-sized pieces. Add the chicken pieces and the seasonings to the pan. Turn the heat to medium-low.

In a cup, stir the flour into the cold milk until there are no lumps. Then slowly stir this mixture into the pan to thicken the gravy. Turn the heat to simmer after the mixture comes to a bubble.

Topping

The tube of bread-stick dough comes as 8 highly pliable strips that you may sculpt any way you want before you bake them. Kids might love the dough/biscuit baked in the shape of their initials or a heart. Or roll the dough strips up like a snail and stick a small piece of Monterey Jack cheese in the very middle. It's playtime, and you can do what you want to.

(Continued)

Arrange your flour artwork on an ungreased cookie sheet. Time the baking according to package directions—probably about 15 minutes.

Stir the barely simmering stew occasionally as the topping bakes. Serve in shallow soup bowls topped with a baked "dumpling."

This is a meal in itself, though some might appreciate a salad.

Dumpling lovers: If you prefer real dumplings boiled on top of a stew instead of the bread-stick-dough method above, use biscuit-mix dough and follow the package directions for dumplings. Add the dumplings right after you've thickened the gravy.

Serves 4–5.

Turkey Tetons

You who took French may know that *tetons* is the word for "breasts," which is why those big mountains in Wyoming are called the Grand Tetons. Well, turkeys have rather grand tetons, too, and that part is what we are cooking tonight. This dish must be started at least an hour and a half before you want to eat, but the actual hands-on preparation time is about 10 minutes.

This particular turkey is not like your boring Pilgrim bird. It has a daring Hispanic flavor and will be loved by all who like Mexican food. It is festive enough for special occasions.

I have not yet found anyone who doesn't like this.

1 turkey breast (about 3 pounds)	1 clove garlic, minced
2 large onions, sliced	2 teaspoons dried oregano
1¹/₂ cups orange juice	2 teaspoons cumin seeds or dried cumin
¹/₂ cup tequila (or lime juice)	Salt to taste

Stick the turkey in an oiled baking pan and roast at 425° for 30 minutes. Then throw all the other ingredients over the turkey. Cover the baking pan with foil or a cover and roast another hour at 350°. (Be sure to turn down the heat.)

After an hour, uncover and cook a little longer, until the turkey skin gets crisp. Baste occasionally with the gravy/juice.

Give your dinner visual sparkle by serving the turkey sliced on a platter, surrounded by its natural gravy with a ridge of warmed black beans spooned down the center of the slices. Sprinkle some chopped cilantro on the beans. Put some fresh salsa on the side. Add warm tortillas and a green salad, and you have yourself a special dinner, something to celebrate a family event—a new job, a college acceptance, a farewell to your kid's probation officer.

Serves 4.

Parmesan-Broiled Fish

This simple, fast recipe is a faux fish fry. The coating and broiling make the fish taste as though it is deep-fried—where are those hush puppies?—but in fact, it's simply broiled. This is what to do with your local fish fillets, whether the fish is catfish, trout, scrod, snapper, halibut or fill-in-the-blank.

This recipe works for thinner fish fillets only. Cook those those thick slabs of tuna and swordfish some other way.

1 cup grated Parmesan cheese
4 tablespoons cornmeal
1¹/₂ teaspoons paprika
¹/₈ teaspoon ground red pepper
2 eggs, beaten

4 4-ounce fish fillets
Salt to taste

Topping
Mayonnaise or tartar sauce

Heat the broiler.

In a large zip-top bag, combine the cheese, cornmeal, paprika and pepper. Beat the two eggs with a fork. Place the fish fillets, one by one, in the egg mixture, coating both sides. Add the fish to the cheese-and-cornmeal bag. Seal and shake to cover.

Take the fish out of the bag. Spray a broiler pan with vegetable oil so it's easy to clean up. Broil the fillets about 3¹/₂ minutes on each side or until cooked all the way through. Place the fish about one-third of the way from the top of the oven, not right under the broiler. Watch closely and turn as soon as the fish begins to get quite brown. If it's browning too fast, put the pan down near the bottom of the oven.

Salt to taste. Top with a dollop of low-fat mayo or tartar sauce.

As for side dishes, corn on the cob would not be refused, nor a green salad with chunks of sweet yellow and red peppers.

Serves 4 if your particular 4 are satisfied with one fillet each.

Light Marinated Shrimp

An easy make-ahead recipe, this versatile dish can be a light and cool dinner for 6 or, with minor modifications, even a star dish on the cocktail-buffet circuit. About the only way you can go wrong is to make the shrimp too far ahead—say, the day before. Then the shrimp get too soft. But do give these at least 2 to 4 hours in their marinating bath.

If making this for a family dinner, follow the recipe below exactly, using the already-cooked small shrimp and the chopped mushrooms. However, if it's party hors d'oeuvres you're after, at least double the dish and make it with medium cooked-and-cleaned shrimp and bite-sized whole sautéed mushrooms—all to be speared by a toothpick.

In either case, drain the marinade before serving.

1¹/₂ pounds cooked small shrimp (about 3 cups)
12 large mushrooms, finely chopped
4 green onions, finely chopped (green and white parts)
4 stalks celery, finely chopped

Marinade
6 tablespoons rice wine vinegar
2 tablespoons soy sauce

4 teaspoons sesame oil (don't omit)
1 teaspoon freshly grated ginger
¹/₈ teaspoon sugar
Salt and pepper to taste

Garnish
Cilantro

In a large bowl, gently mix the cooked shrimp with the chopped mushrooms, scallions and celery. In a smaller bowl, mix the marinade ingredients together. Pour the marinade over the shrimp mixture. Cover and refrigerate. For dinner, drain the shrimp mixture and serve chilled on a bed of mixed baby lettuces with thinly sliced, salted cucumbers on the side. A round of hot bread and a tomato, basil and sliced mozzarella salad will round out the meal. Sure it's mixing Chinese and Italian cuisine, but if Marco Polo can, so can you.

Cocktail-Buffet Recipe
Use whole medium cooked-and-cleaned shrimp and whole bite-sized mushrooms. The marinade is the same.

Serves 6.

Tuna Revisited

When the history of the tuna casserole is written, scholars will note a definite fall from favor in the late twentieth century. Just the word "casserole" evokes the image of a culinary fuddy-duddy.

History should take another look, because casseroles can be delicious, are often easy and are almost always comforting. And the tuna casserole of the 1950s—our foremothers' answer to the call of the menu—deserves a retrospective.

But until that happens, here is a tuna dish for today. This recipe is very fast—no baking. Mild cheese has been added for flavor.

¹/₂ pound elbow macaroni	**²/₃ cup grated Monterey Jack cheese**
2 tablespoons butter	**6¹/₂-ounce can tuna in spring water**
2 tablespoons flour	**2-ounce jar sliced pimentos**
1 cup milk	**Salt and pepper to taste**

Cook the macaroni in a large pot of boiling, salted water about 7 minutes. Start timing when the water comes to a boil after the macaroni has been added. Drain well when done.

As the macaroni boils, melt the butter over low heat using a large, heavy frying pan. Add the flour, stirring constantly for about 2 minutes.

Next, slowly whisk the milk into the flour mixture, turning the heat to medium high. Bring to a boil, still stirring so nothing burns or lumps.

When the sauce thickens, add the grated cheese. Stir over low heat until the cheese melts. Then add the tuna, which has been forked into bite-sized chunks. Stir carefully until the tuna is warmed. Season with salt and pepper. Add the pimentos for a color spark.

Last, add the pasta. Stir to coat with the sauce.

Serve right away. Peas on the side along with some crisp vegetable sticks (carrot, celery or cucumbers) would finish things nicely.

Serves 3–4.

Scallops for Fussbudgets

Scallops are guerrilla food because they cook almost instantly with no waste of motion or material. There are no bones. There is no skin or fat. However, when my four kids were growing up, scallops were a hard sell. Had I this recipe in hand, things might have been different.

The recipe may sound weird. The scallops are sautéed in orange juice, among other things—but they taste good. Another plus: the juice in the pan looks like butter, so if you don't have your glasses on, you may think you are eating lots of buttery stuff. In fact, it is an illusion. Total fat per person is $1/4$ teaspoon, so this dish is especially good when you are trying to take off pounds but don't want to feel deprived.

If you have fresh tarragon on hand, use it.

Because there's not much cooking fat, use your nonstick pan.

$1/2$ **teaspoon cooking oil**
$1/2$ **teaspoon butter**
$1/4$ **cup fresh orange juice**
$1/4$ **cup white wine**

**1 teaspoon fresh tarragon
(or $1/2$ teaspoon dried)**
1 pound small scallops

Melt the oil and butter in a large frying pan over medium-high heat. Add the orange juice, wine and tarragon. Stir. Add the scallops, cooking a few minutes until the scallops are opaque. Remove the scallops and boil down the sauce a bit. Pour the sauce over the scallops. Garnish with tarragon.

Fill out the meal with a favorite vegetable and couscous, a small, easily cooked grain.

Serves 4.

Scallop Puffs

This is good, fast and different—easy to do, easy to eat. It's the perfect light supper or even a ladies' lunch, should such a luxurious event still exist in the world. Try it with wild rice pilaf (from a packaged mix) and steamed asparagus. Be sure the "meringue" topping on the scallops is cooked through.

1 pound small scallops
1 cup water
1/4 cup light mayonnaise
1 tablespoon freshly minced parsley

1 tablespoon fresh chives
1/2 teaspoon soy sauce
1 egg white, stiffly beaten

In a covered pot, simmer the scallops for a few minutes in the cup of water until they turn opaque. Drain well or the dish will be watery. Cool.

Meanwhile, make the topping: Mix the mayonnaise with the parsley, chives and soy sauce. Beat the egg white until stiff and fold it into the mayo mixture. Put the scallops into a serving casserole that can take the high heat of a broiler. Top the scallops with the mayo mixture and put the casserole on a low rack under the hot broiler.

Broil a few minutes until the topping is thoroughly cooked and light brown. Don't leave broiler watch.

Sometimes, when I just have myself to please, I serve the scallops in the middle of a big plate of mixed greens. The hot scallops and cool greens make a nice contrast.

Serves 2–3.

Don't Buy into Impossible Expectations

The Assumption of a Posh Nosh

Some cookbook writers seem to assume we're the silver-spooned rich wondering what amusing thing to serve on cook's night off. We, on the other hand, know the truth: Only pizza and peanut butter are between us and starvation. And because fancy cookbooks don't relate to the real-life nature of American eating, they leave us with too many elaborate recipes on our shelves and no idea of what to cook tonight.

So then we get indecisive. We turn into Pantry Statues, frozen in front of the cupboard wondering what to choose for dinner—what to make that will bring us up to the level of our own inflated expectations. And because we then tire of the whole process, we turn away from home cooking and solve the dinner dilemma by one of two outs: take-out or go-out.

For most of us, though, these solutions are not possible seven nights a week. So what to do?

First, reduce your expectations. Do not buy into the notion that life without truffle soufflé is no life at all. It isn't true. Mother Teresa has led a good, albeit truffleless, life. And even if you can't be a marvelous chef in your spare time, you are still a valuable person.

Think about it. Martha Stewart's *job* is to be Martha Stewart. She gets paid well to make castles out of gingerbread. If somebody paid you to do that, you'd probably turn into a darn fine cookie architect, too.

But she's not the only one prompting our culinary inferiority complex. For instance, our television culture has been invaded by people in white coats carrying sharp kitchen knives. Run fast, my dears, it's the invasion of the PBS chefs. They chop, sizzle, sauté, flame, grind and process food, always raising the unspoken question: Why aren't you chopping, sizzling and so forth yourself?

Again, if it were your paid job, you would. But it's a sideline for you, something you were drafted to do by circumstance or gender. It's a wonder most of us home cooks do as well as we do, considering that we never signed up for the culinary life in the first place.

The way out here is to *refuse to buy into outdated ideas,* such as:

- ➡ It is your duty to be a gourmet chef.
- ➡ Cooking must always be taken seriously.
- ➡ All things must be cooked from scratch.

- ➡ **Fancy cooking is a way to compete and establish oneself socially.**

- ➡ **Cooking equals loving: i.e., "Nothing says lovin' like something from the oven."**

Guerrilla cooks, however, believe none of the above. In fact, we think that nothing says loving like something from a restaurant menu.

2 **Daily Dinner:**

More Ways Out

THE ARSENIC HOUR

The Arsenic Hour

Why is dinner such a pain?

Because it's the worst time of day to attempt anything—nuclear physics or cooking.

People are tired and cranky. Blood-sugar levels are low. The kids, if there are kids, are probably home with their latchkeys still around their necks. You yourself may never have gotten near a real lunch.

So what's for dinner? And when will it be ready? And oh, no, not fish sticks again. And Bobby, don't eat that, you'll spoil your appetite.

And then you, the designated cook, think to yourself: Just what dinner is it that I'm talking about?

My friend Cynthia calls this time The Arsenic Hour.

Now the way to get through The Arsenic Hour is to appease the obviously starving with a healthy snack that won't spoil their dinners.

Oreos.

Okay, maybe not Oreos. But the usual crisp vegetable snacks—crudité—take time and patience to prepare. Wash, peel, chop, etc. One obvious out is the prepackaged, store-bought vegetable. But these often have have a funny texture and taste—for instance, faux carrots doing a bad carrot imitation.

Fruit has emerged over the years as the answer at my house. My kids, culinary free-thinkers all, simply polished the dessert off in the kitchen before anyone even sat down for the meal.

A cold apple, a perfectly ripe pear—these are the little salvations that can keep a family going until the meat loaf appears. With fruit as an appetizer, nobody cooks. Nobody peels or chops. No mess to clean. Blood sugar up, workload down.

Yes, you may have to face criticism that you're doing everything backward, but culinary rules are arbitrary. Tell your critics that the laws of the table change from age to age. In the eighteenth century, for example, sweet puddings often were the first course. Even in the middle of the twentieth century, fancy meals "out" used to start with sherbet or fruit cocktail. So what if you do things backward, according to today's culinary rules? If it works, stick to your bananas.

Now that the fruit issue has been settled, let us proceed to the actual dinner, which in this chapter, will take the form of meats, dinner soups and easy cheats such as hearty breakfast goodies for supper. Some food writers would chat up these meals as "man-pleasing," but the cookperson in the nonsexist guerrilla kitchen would describe them as just good.

The Giant Guerrilla Cheeseburger

Take your eating audience by surprise with a hefty variation on the cheeseburger, this one made with nonfat cheese. We are talking mega-burger here, one huge meat patty on a giant "roll," which is, in fact, a store-bought unsliced bread round about 8" across. Just one of these burgers serves six when cut into wedges.

The key to success with this recipe is choosing good bread. Buy a fresh round of bread that has some softness and give to it, rather than a very hard, dense kind of loaf.

One other important thing is to add the nonfat cheese at the last minute and to turn the oven down when you do. Nonfat cheeses melt better at lower temperatures.

This recipe is made for Friday night family dinner.

You should also serve it to kid guests so they can go home and tell their mothers what a great cook you are. Actually, this is a good grown-up treat, too.

The Cheeseburger

1 1/2 pounds ground beef

1 small onion, finely chopped (about 1/2 cup)

1 tablespoon mustard

1 tablespoon prepared horseradish, drained

1/2 teaspoon salt

1/3 cup chili sauce or ketchup

1 cup nonfat grated cheddar cheese

The Roll

1 round loaf of Italian or sourdough bread, unsliced

Whipped butter and mustard to taste

Heat the oven to 350°.

Mix the first five ingredients together. Put this seasoned meat mixture into an ungreased pie plate. Or mix the ingredients right in the pie plate and then clean up the sides of the plate. This tactic saves washing a dish.

Then, with the meat spread evenly over the bottom surface of the pie plate, put the chili sauce or ketchup on top and bake uncovered 45 minutes. Set a timer.

Slice the bread round in half horizontally. Spread low-fat whipped butter on one side and slather a favorite mustard on the other. (I use hot 'n sweet mustard, but it doesn't matter.) Put the halves, dough side up, on a cookie sheet.

When the 45-minute timer for the meat rings, turn the heat down to 300° and slide the bread halves into the oven. At the same time, take the meat out, drain off any fat and sprinkle on the cheese. Return to the oven. Set the timer for 5 minutes.

After 5 minutes, pull out the meat. Turn off the oven. Let the bread stay warm in the oven.

Allow the meat to rest on the counter for another 5 minutes. Then slide the burger onto the bread bottom. Add whatever you like: lettuce, thinly sliced tomatoes, onions or nothing at all. Top with the other half of the bread round. Cut with a serrated bread knife.

This is super-good and filling. And it has what every good guerrilla needs: the element of surprise. This is no ordinary burger.

For special kids or special events, insert toothpicks with colorful paper frills into each sky-high wedge.

Serves 6.

Shortcut Shepherd's Pie

Also known as Cottage Pie, this is a cozy food: mashed potatoes layered over juicy meat bits and then baked. The meat under the mashed potatoes varies from region to region. This quick version features always-popular ground chuck or, as it was known in my family, hungerburger.

Try this dish when you feel down and out, and don't be afraid of the instant mashed potatoes. They are delicious.

Don't be afraid of the dried soup, either. Dehydration methods have improved. This soup mix has actual vegetables with real color and flavors, unlike the dried soups and gravy mixes that are all flour, MSG, sugar, salt and dyes.

The Meat Layer

1 pound ground beef

1 onion, minced

1 package dried spring-vegetable soup

1^1/$_2$ cups water

The Mashed-Potato Topping

2^2/$_3$ cups instant mashed potatoes

2^2/$_3$ cups water

1 cup milk

2 tablespoons butter

Salt and pepper to taste

Heat the oven to 350°.

Brown the meat and the sliced onion in a large nonstick skillet over medium-high heat. If the skillet is one that can also go in the oven to bake, it will save washing a serving dish.

Now, while the meat and onions are browning, make up the potatoes. Heat the water, milk and butter over low heat just to boiling. Then take them off the heat and add the potatoes, mixing well.

The potatoes quickly done, go back to the meat mixture. Add the soup mix and 1^1/$_2$ cups water to the meat, stirring until mixed.

Now you can either transfer the meat mixture to a pie plate and top with the potatoes or, if you are working with a skillet that can go in the oven—say a cast-iron frying pan—just dump the potatoes on top of the meat.

Make a crisscross pattern by dragging fork tines across the potato landscape. Season the topping with salt and pepper to taste.

Bake for 30 minutes or until you can see or hear the juices bubbling. If you want the top really browned, put the pan *briefly* under a hot broiler. Watch the browning. Don't leave your post at the oven door.

Green peas are a traditional side dish. Make the peas rare rather than medium or well-done. A salad of sliced beets and curly endive would be nice.

Vegetarians can do their own thing with a shepherd's pie, using seasoned and stir-fried corn kernels, mushrooms, peppers, tomatoes and onions as the "meat" layer.

Serves pure comfort to 4 people. Alternatively, it will serve 2 people who are very hungry.

New Age Beef Stroganoff

Beef Stroganoff was the dining-out dish of the mid-twentieth century, but worries about the fat in the sour cream sent this meal into culinary obscurity. With the recent revival of sour cream—the palatable nonfat version—it's time to try beef Stroganoff again. This is easy and elegant—appropriate for either family dining or entertaining.

1 pound lean beef round steak	**1 cup nonfat sour cream**
3/4 pound mushrooms	**2 tablespoons tomato paste (or ketchup)**
1 tablespoon cooking oil	**Salt and ground pepper**

Cut the beef very thinly on the bias (which means on a slant, not straight up and down.) Wash the mushrooms and slice them thinly.

Heat the oil in a nonstick skillet. Add the meat and cook over high heat, stirring for about 3 minutes. Add the mushrooms and stir more, another 3 or so minutes. Add the sour cream and tomato paste, bravely using ketchup if you're really in a hurry. (It works. Ketchup is just semiliquid tomato paste with a little sweetening.)   (*Continued*)

Finish with salt and pepper.

Present with a green salad featuring many different kinds of colorful vegetables: fresh shredded carrots, red onions, lightly steamed broccoli bits.

Serves 4 theoretically, but 2 enthusiastic test eaters have polished off the whole thing.

To clean mushrooms quickly, forget the strainer or, heaven forbid, the mushroom brush. Just let water run into a plastic bag full of mushrooms—enough to cover them. Then, holding the top closed, jiggle the bag, which jiggles the mushrooms, which jiggles the dirt off. Next, poke a hole in the bottom of the bag to let the water run out. Violà, clean mushrooms. Wash quickly, so the mushrooms won't soak in the water.

Killer Meat Loaf

Many are the meat-loaf cravings of man. Because the meat is baked in the shape of a loaf of bread, this dish is a good choice for hesitant carnivores or recovering vegetarians. No bones to confront. Everything more or less prechewed by a grinder.

This simple version, my favorite, is topped with chili sauce or salsa. It also is flecked with oatmeal: The cereal lightens the loaf. No more stone-heavy meatbricks. I like to make this on a Saturday morning, letting the uncooked loaf mellow in the refrigerator until it's shoved in the oven for Saturday supper.

Meat loaf and a good video—another wild Saturday night.

Meat Loaf

1 pound ground beef

6-ounce can tomato paste

$1/2$ cup oatmeal

4 tablespoons fine bread crumbs (or bran or wheat germ)

3 tablespoons chopped celery

1 onion, chopped

1 egg, beaten

2 cloves garlic, minced

Salt and pepper to taste

Topping

Salsa, chili sauce or ketchup

Heat the oven to 350°.

Put all the ingredients, except the topping, in a meat-loaf pan. Mix the ingredients together with your fingers. Note: You are mixing the ingredients right in the pan, so clean up the sides of the pan with a paper towel before baking.

Top with a layer of drained salsa, chili sauce or ketchup.

Bake for 50 to 60 minutes, but no longer. Longer will make it tough. Serve hot, maybe with green beans and wild rice.

If there are leftover meat-loaf slices, use them in sandwiches.

Serves 4.

Steak in a Bag

Dinner for a small crowd is literally in the bag when you get home from work if, in the morning, you put a flank steak in a big plastic bag full of marinade. Then it's flavored by the end of the day. So you just broil the steak, and dinner is done without doing you in.

The marinade has two special ingredients: Chinese five-spice powder, which you can pick up in the Asian-food section of your supermarket, and—believe it or not—Earl Grey tea bags.

This is also a great marinade for poultry.

The Marinade
2 cups water
1 cup teriyaki sauce
1 teaspoon ground black pepper
1/2 cup dark molasses

1 teaspoon five-spice powder
2 Earl Grey tea bags

The Steak
2 pounds flank steak (or London broil)

To make the marinade, combine the water, teriyaki sauce, black pepper, molasses and five-spice powder in a saucepan. Bring to a boil. Add the tea bags. Let sit until cool, then remove tea bags.

Put the steak in a big zip-top plastic bag. Add the marinade. Seal tightly. Refrigerate.

At dinnertime, take the steak out of the bag and broil it in the kitchen or grill it outside under the stars.

Good with sliced ripe tomatoes, sautéed mushrooms and a big round of hot bread.

Serves 6.

Two for One—A Second Act of Chicken

If you have guests coming soon, double the marinade recipe, use half on the steak, and reserve the rest—*unused*—as a marinade for the next weekend's party poultry. At that time, grill the marinated chicken. Serve with rice, snow peas and a green salad topped with sliced water chestnuts and red peppers. Try a colorful fruit sorbet with chopped candied ginger on top for dessert.

Note: Don't taste the marinade after raw food has been sitting in it.

Baked Pork Tenderloin

Health-conscious people have a real prejudice against pork. They assume that it must be loaded with fat. But have they ever met a pork tenderloin, a boneless cylinder of lean meat that's less fattening than a chicken leg with the skin on? If you aren't familiar with pork tenderloin, imagine a round piece of lean Canadian bacon. Canadian bacon is pork tenderloin that's been smoked, flavored and sliced.

1/4 cup ketchup

1 teaspoon brown sugar (white is okay, too)

2 tablespoons water

2 tablespoons hoisin sauce (found in Asian food section)

1/2 teaspoon salt

2 cloves garlic, minced

1 pork tenderloin, about 11/2 pounds

The pork may come two pieces to a package, rather than one, each about 3/4 pounds. It makes no difference. Use both. Leftovers make great sandwiches.

In a shallow dish, mix all the ingredients except the pork. Add the pork and coat on all sides with the marinade. You can let the pork soak a minimum of 1 hour or up to 24 hours, turning if you remember.

(Continued)

Heat the oven to 425°. Place the pork on a rack in a roasting pan. Roast uncovered about 55 minutes or until a thermometer inserted into the thickest part reads at least 160°. I like pork cooked until the thermometer hits 180 or above, with no pink in the middle at all.

Swab with a bit of the marinade about halfway through cooking.

Try the pork with whipped sweet potatoes. Cook 2 large sweet potatoes 13 to 15 minutes in the microwave. Cool, scoop out, mash and salt.

This main dish is also good with steamed green beans that have a bit of pickle juice poured over them.

Serves 6.

Guerrilla Tip

Instead of worrying about making a sauce for vegetables or dousing them with pounds of butter, look to your spice shelf or to items already in the refrigerator. Pickle juice on string beans is just one variation. Also try nutmeg on carrots, cinnamon on sweet potatoes, sweet-and-hot mustard on cauliflower, tarragon on peas, salsa on baked potatoes, rosemary on roasted red potatoes, chopped black olives scattered over red peppers, small cocktail onions mixed with peas, walnuts mixed into eggplant, sesame oil shaken over bok choy, a bit of barbecue sauce to enliven corn bits, nutmeg on spinach, red wine vinegar over beets, American cheese slices melted over broccoli, a touch of maple syrup on carrots, warmed mayonnaise over potatoes, pimentos over zucchini.

Bowls full of interesting soups are just fine for dinner if they feature something you can get your teeth around, like pasta or hefty toppings made of corn bread, pastry or pie crust. Here are a few candidates for two-fisted family feeding.

Corn Chowder in Four Colors

A 10-minute dish that manages to combine gutsiness with good looks, this dish could become a household favorite. The good looks come from the colors: the yellow of corn, the creamy white of potatoes, the green of scallions and the pink of a few bits of bacon. The taste will appeal especially to those who wish they could consume an entire can of creamed corn when nobody is looking.

The meat-aversive cook can leave out the Canadian bacon. Bacon lovers can double the amount.

This recipe uses the frozen potatoes meant to be used for hash browns. These are good in soup. Get a big 2-pound sack of the chopped, frozen, unflavored potatoes meant for hash browns—*not* the hash-brown patties. Use half the sack for this recipe and store the rest for the next time you need a quick potato rescue.

1 cup water
1 cup milk (or half-and-half)
1 pound frozen hash-brown potatoes (about 4 cups)
17-ounce can creamed corn

¹/₂ cup green onions, chopped
2 slices Canadian bacon, chopped
Salt and ground pepper

Put the water and milk in a large saucepan. Bring to a boil. Meanwhile, chop the onions and bacon slices and open the can of creamed corn. When the water/milk mixture comes

(Continued)

to a boil, add the potatoes. Break up any large potato chunks. Stir a minute or so, until all is bubbly. Then add the corn, onions, bacon, salt and pepper. Stir to mix. Cover and lower heat to simmer. The chowder will take about 8 minutes to simmer.

A first-course salad topped with chilled canned sliced beets would be good.

Serves about 4.

When cooking this recipe, reclose the opened package of potatoes with a clothespin. Clothespins work well to fasten opened sacks of frozen foods. They also will reclose sacks of potato chips, pasta, chocolate chips, etc. Also useful as closers: rubber bands and twist ties.

Chili Under a Corn Bread Blanket

Chili is an across-the-board people pleaser. You can make chili from scratch on a lazy Saturday afternoon, or you can go out to the latest movie and make this. It's quick and, yes, it has a canned-bean base. But don't sneer at using canned chili until you've tried the newer versions. They now come in an array of choices: chicken chili, onion chili, chunky chili, and so forth. You can do a meat chili or you can go entirely veggie.

The baked corn bread blanketing the chili makes this dish special. The slightly sweet topping contrasts nicely with the warm spiciness of the chili. Put bowls of nonfat sour cream and salsa on the table to pile on top of the corn bread and chili.

1 onion, sliced

1 tablespoon cooking oil

2 15-ounce cans chili

1/3 cup of your favorite bottled barbecue sauce

15-ounce package corn bread, mixed according to directions

Heat the oven to 400°.

For a simple bake-and-serve presentation, use a microwavable, ovenproof casserole that holds about 2 quarts. Put the onion and oil in the dish. Microwave for 3 minutes. (You can cook the onion on the stovetop in a pot, but why dirty another dish?)

Remove the casserole from the microwave. Add the chili and barbecue sauce. Mix with a gentle hand so the beans won't get mashed.

Prepare the corn bread batter, following package directions exactly. Most mixes require water or an egg and water.

Slowly pour the batter over the chili in the casserole. Bake uncovered for about 35–40 minutes, or until the center of the corn bread is firm. Best hot from the oven.

Good with a green salad topped with chopped cilantro, sliced tomatoes and avocado.

Serves 4–6.

Taco Soup

This may be the easiest supper you ever prepared. There's no real cooking, just warming. This is a hot item on the junior culinary circuit, and I have not tampered with its brilliant simplicity. After all, I was a mother once. Actually, I was a mother four times and wish I had this recipe then. (I am now a Mother Emeritus and so can eat higher on the food chain—above the tacos, but still well below the caviar.)

49 1/2-ounce can chicken broth

28-ounce can diced tomatoes (with juice)

16-ounce bag frozen corn kernels

3 cups tortilla chips

3 cups shredded nonfat Monterey Jack cheese

Throw the chicken broth, tomatoes (with juice) and corn into a large pot. Bring to a boil and then simmer for about 5 minutes.

Get out your soup plates and put a handful of chips on the plates. Ladle the soup over the chips. Sprinkle the cheese over the top.

Don't serve this soup until all the folks are assembled. You don't want the chips to get soggy.

Serves 6.

Drunken Onion Soup

Onion soup is the chicken broth of the intellectual.

The rest of us like it, too.

This light onion soup is made with chicken broth. There's never any left, so it must be good. If you chill the onions in the produce drawer before peeling them, you'll get off easy in the tears department. When marketing, try to find onions that aren't old, soft or bin-weary.

The soup has a bread-and-cheese topping, but it can also stand alone.

The Soup
4 large, fresh yellow onions, thinly sliced
2 tablespoons cooking oil
49$^1/_2$-ounce can chicken broth
$^1/_4$ cup dry sherry (optional but good)

The Topping
1 cup grated Monterey Jack cheese
4 pieces lightly toasted bread

Peel and slice the onions. Heat the oil in a soup pot over medium-high. Throw in the sliced onions and stir occasionally until they are soft and definitely browned at the edges—perhaps 7 minutes. (The browning adds greatly to the flavor.) Add the chicken broth and sherry. Bring to a boil and then run at a sturdy simmer for 15 minutes.

Meanwhile, grate the cheese and lightly toast four slices of French bread or almost any hefty peasant bread. To fancy up the presentation, use the rim of a glass to cut a toast round out of the bread slice.

Ladle the soup into bowls that can go under the broiler. Top with the bread and then the cheese. Place under a hot broiler for 1 or 2 minutes, or until the cheese begins to melt.

If you don't have any flameproof soup bowls, you can pour all of the soup into a heat-proof serving dish and float the bread and cheese on top. Place the dish briefly under a hot broiler and bring to the table to ladle into soup plates.

Try a green salad with romaine and walnuts as a first course. A vinaigrette dressing made with a splash of walnut oil is a nice touch.

Serves 4.

Lazy-Day Clam Chowder

When you grow up in New England, as I did, you know the clam chowder at home is white, chunky with potatoes—and canned. If New Englanders go to the trouble of tracking and digging clams, they are going to steam them whole, not lose them in the bottom of a soup. But, as much as I admire good convenience foods, I think that canned clam chowders often taste embalmed. So here's a perky and fast clam chowder made mostly from fresh ingredients. Just the clams are canned, and a good thing, too—unless you want to scrub, steam, pick over, chop and cook bivalves today.

2 baking potatoes	**8-ounce bottle clam juice**
1 small onion, peeled and sliced	**1 cup milk**
1 tablespoon cooking oil	**6^1/$_2$-ounce can chopped clams,** *drained*
2 slices Canadian bacon, chopped (optional but tasty)	

Wash two baking potatoes. Prick and microwave for 9 minutes or until done. Of course, you can bake them in the oven for 1 hour at 400°, but the chowder won't taste any better with oven-baked potatoes.

Sauté the sliced onions in oil in a saucepan. Add the chopped bacon and stir.

Remove the potatoes from the microwave (or oven). Split to cool. When cooler to the touch, scoop out the potato from the skin, forking it into edible bits. Don't worry if some skin gets mixed up with the rest. A bit of skin gives the chowder texture.

Put the potato bits in the saucepan with the onions and bacon. Add the clam juice and milk. Mix and warm slowly over low heat, scraping the bottom so the soup won't burn.

If it does begin to scorch because you were called into action elsewhere, get that soup out of the pot before the burned flavor hits the whole batch. Many a milk-warming project can be saved by this quick action.

Add the drained can of clams at the last minute.

Serve with old-fashioned chowder crackers plus carrot and bell pepper vegetable sticks.

Serves 2 for dinner. Just increase the ingredients proportionately if you want more chowder, letting the potatoes run longer in the microwave. Four potatoes may take 18–20 minutes to micro-cook.

Smoked Chicken, Pasta and Spinach Salad

Anyone you serve this pasta to should kneel and kiss the hem of your jeans. This is delicious—a dish to prove what a fine culinary touch you can display when the mood hits.

However, this recipe does not take a long time. For instance, a package of already-washed spinach plus an already-cooked smoked chicken give the cook a head start. And 1/2 pound of *small* pasta bits can be cooked rapidly in just 6 cups of water, rather than waiting for that big pasta pot to boil.

The special dressing is important to the success of the dish. This recipe makes about three times more than you'll need. It keeps in the refrigerator and can be used on many a salad over the next few weeks.

The Salad

6 cups water

1/2 pound small pasta (orzo, farfalline or your favorite)

1 smoked chicken, about 2 1/2 pounds, meat taken off bones and sliced

1 large package spinach leaves, already washed

1/2 cup Poppy Seed Dressing (next column)

2 slices Canadian bacon, diced

The Dressing

1 cup salad oil

1/2 cup cranberry juice

1 teaspoon salt

1 tablespoon honey

1 tablespoon grated white or yellow onion

1 tablespoon poppy seeds

Salt and pepper to taste

Put 6 cups of water in a saucepan and when the water boils, add the small pasta. Cook according to package directions. Meanwhile, pull the meat off the chicken and slice.

For the dressing, mix all the ingredients except the poppy seeds. When the ingredients are well combined, add the poppy seeds. Stir again. (*Continued*)

Drain the pasta. Put the spinach on the bottom of the serving bowl or platter. (A clear glass salad bowl makes a nice presentation.) Add the pasta and then the chicken. Micro-cook the diced bacon 1 minute in the microwave and throw it on top.

Bring the dressing to the table and gently mix all the ingredients in front of your eating audience.

Present with a basket full of hot bread sticks.

This recipe is fun to tinker with. Suggestions: more pasta and less spinach (use a regular large pasta pot if you're upping the pasta proportions), more spinach and less pasta, different pastas and greens, interesting toppings such as homemade croutons made from baguettes of French bread.

Serves 4.

Instant Cold Pasta Salad

There are warm nights when a cold pasta salad would definitely hit the spot. Here's a sneaky shortcut that will put cold "pasta" on the table in a few minutes. The trick is to use Chinese ramen noodles, which cook in 3 minutes. Just rinse them in very cold water, drain well and you have a delicious base for cold pasta salad.

Dried ramen noodles are usually found near the soups or in the Asian food section of your supermarket.

Serve the noodles with one of the topping combinations below or with your favorite protein: shrimp, crab bits, diced chicken. Moisten the protein of choice with a bit of mayonnaise. This pasta is also good as a side dish.

3 packages ramen noodle soup mix   **Salt and pepper to taste**
6 cups water

Bring 6 cups of water to a boil. Add the ramen noodles, breaking into pieces. DO NOT USE THE SEASONING MIX. Boil the noodles 3 minutes (or according to package directions). Rinse in very cold water. Shake to drain well.

Suggested topping combinations:

➡ Tuna chunks, pimentos, capers, green onions and mayonnaise

➡ Sautéed bell peppers (yellow, red, green)

➡ Chopped ham and fresh peas

Serves 4.

Guerrilla Tip

This guerrilla pasta solution is good when you're eating solo and don't want to get a big deal going with the pasta pot. It is also good used as hot pasta. Simply rinse the cooked noodles in really hot water instead of cold and proceed to top according to your preference. Just olive oil, salt and grated cheese would be fine.

Steak-and-Caesar Salad

This recipe pleases most of the people most of the time: Thin slices of thick broiled steak sit atop romaine leaves, the whole dressed up with freshly grated Parmesan and warm croutons. Salad eaters get their innings here while the blood lust of steak eaters is also satisfied. This dish can go from thought to table in about 20 minutes.

You can make your own Caesar salad from scratch if it pleases you, but this recipe assumes that you are bushed and low on dinner energy. It uses one of the fresh-packaged Caesar-salad lettuce mixes now on the market, complete with croutons and dressing in a packet.

1 pound boneless top sirloin, 1" thick

Salt and pepper to taste

1 package Caesar salad mix, including dressing and croutons

$1/2$ cup Parmesan cheese, grated

Heat broiler. Broil the steak about 15 minutes—about $7^{1}/_{2}$ minutes per side, until the meat reaches at least 160° or the desired state of doneness. Be sure to turn once. Salt and pepper to taste. Cut the meat thinly across the grain—not straight up and down, but on a slant. Of course, you can grill the steak outside on the barbie and you can also upgrade to filet mignon if you're feeling fancy.

While the meat cooks, open the package of salad mix and shake the lettuce into a serving bowl. Add the inner leaves of your own romaine if you need to fluff out the amount. Free the croutons from their package and put them in a microwavable bowl. Just before serving, microwave them for 45 seconds so they'll be nice and warm.

Toss the salad with the dressing. Add the warm croutons. Add the thinly sliced steak to the top and sprinkle on the Parmesan to finish the dish.

Serves 4.

There are several points of view about Parmesan cheese. One is that only one Parmesan amounts to much: Parmigiano-Reggiano from Italy. It is often shaved into wafer-thin slices, rather than shredded. On the other end of the spectrum, there are those who are content to shake very old and dusty "Parmesan" out of a can onto their spaghetti.

The guerrilla cook notes that Parmigiano-Reggiano is not found in all markets and is, in fact, expensive and very hard to grate and shave. On the other hand, the stuff in shaker cans seems to lack taste, which is really the main point of a grated-cheese topping.

Try this compromise for daily dinners. Look for the already-grated Parmesan in plastic tubs in the dairy case. Also good are the pre-grated Asiago and Romano cheeses. Brands differ greatly, so experiment.

Shortcut Chinese Chicken Salad

Start with a store-bought roasted chicken, and you are halfway to a good dinner salad. Just pull the chicken meat off the bones and cut it into bite-sized shreds to mix with the greens. For crunch, use whole almonds—smoked if you can get them—along with a scattering of chow-mein noodles. You can use bottled sesame salad dressing, but the taste and feel of most bottled dressings leave a lot to be desired. So try the quick salad dressing below.

The Salad

3/4–1 pound boneless cooked chicken meat

1 head romaine lettuce, shredded

4 green onions, finely chopped

1/2 cup whole almonds (hickory smoked)

1/2 to 1 cup chow mein noodles

Chinese Salad Dressing (below)

Pull the chicken into shreds—it's a good way to let off the day's steam. Cut the lettuce into thin strips and put it in a large serving bowl. Chop up the green onions, whites and all. Mix in with the lettuce. Add the chicken. Drizzle with dressing. Top with chopped nuts and crisp noodle bits. Nice touch: Warm the nuts and chow mein noodles on a plate in the microwave for 1 or 2 minutes.

(Continued)

The Chinese Salad Dressing

When by myself and in a hurry, I often dress salads with a few shakes of teriyaki sauce. Nothing else. Try to find a brand of teriyaki sauce that contains wine, garlic and ginger.

If you want a bit more than that, the following simple recipe has more oomph than many more elaborate dressings.

¹/₄ cup salad oil	**1 teaspoon sesame oil**
¹/₄ cup teriyaki sauce	**Salt and pepper to taste**

Mix together. If you don't use it all, store the remainder in the refrigerator. Later, bring it to room temperature and shake.

Serves 4 as a main dish. Try with big hunks of toasted French-bread baguettes.

Guerrilla Tip

Many are the dinners that can be "made" using store-roasted chicken as a base. Here are some ideas:

➡ **Melt 1 tablespoon butter with 1 tablespoon honey in the microwave. Brush on the warm chicken. Sprinkle with sesame seeds toasted 1 or 2 minutes in the microwave.**

➡ **Warm 1 tablespoon olive oil with the juice of 1 lemon and 1 teaspoon dried tarragon, plus some salt. Brush on the warm chicken.**

➡ **Baste a chicken with barbecue sauce and keep it warm in the oven. Then heat up some canned baked beans, dish out deli coleslaw and add buttermilk biscuits (baked from the refrigerated product in a tube). Put on country music and enjoy.**

Guerrilla French Toast

This is how to wake 'em up with breakfast for dinner. Like all true guerrilla dishes, it's easy—the toast is baked, not fried, so you don't have to slave over a hot range while you flip French toast. This dish also uses what guerrillas love: the element of surprise. The toast is stuffed with jam and, maybe, if you have it on hand, tidbits of berries and other fruits. For the young set, I've made it stuffed with peanut butter and jelly.

Another good point: Guerrilla French Toast is versatile. It can be made in a sweet version, as in this recipe, but if you want to make it stuffed with a thin slice of cheese, simply substitute salt and pepper for the vanilla and cinnamon in the soaking liquid. Then you'll have a heck of a succulent cheese sandwich.

Typically, French toast is fried in lots of butter. Not this version. It will bake crispy golden on a plain cookie sheet that's well-spritzed with butter-flavored cooking spray.

About the only mistake you can make is to try this recipe with thin slices of bread. The slices should be at least 1" thick to take the stuffing. So it's best to buy a whole loaf of bread and slice it yourself.

4 slices *sweet* French bread or challah, 1" thick
4 tablespoons of your favorite jam
2 eggs, beaten

1/2 cup milk
1 teaspoon vanilla extract
1/4 teaspoon cinnamon

First, turn the oven to 375°. This is important.

Second, lay the cut bread slices on the counter and, with a pointed knife, cut into the bottom crust of each slice. But don't cut all the way through the slice. Just make a hole

(Continued)

big enough to get a butter knife full of jam inside. Leave the top and side crusts intact. (This sounds complicated, but it will be obvious what to do just as soon as you stand there looking at the bread with a knife in your hand.)

Stuff each pocket with a tablespoonful of jam. Next, in a shallow pan wide enough to hold all 4 bread slices, mix the eggs, milk, vanilla and cinnamon. Soak the stuffed bread slices for 5 minutes, turning them halfway through.

Now lay the soaked slices in a well-greased baking pan or on a cookie sheet and bake in a preheated 375° oven for 20 minutes. Then, to make sure both sides get crispy, turn them over with a spatula and bake another 5 minutes, or until thoroughly cooked.

Serve hot with lots of fresh fruit and warm maple syrup. Pass a bowl of nonfat yogurt. Try a scoop of nonfat ricotta cheese on each plate. (It looks like ice cream.)

Highly Recommended Variation
Add little bits of fresh ripe fruit along with the jam. Try some blueberries added to each blueberry jam–stuffed pocket, raspberries with raspberry jam or a thin slice of ripe peach with peach preserves.

I could lie and say this will feed 4, but Guerrilla French Toast is so good, 2 people could polish off 4 pieces. When guests come, I double and triple the recipe, figuring 2 slices per adult.

It's smart to delegate cooking chores: Teach your family members how to make this dish so it's their turn next time. In fact, designate each child the czar or czarina of some special dish, whether it's French toast or something else. Have a czar of salads and a czarina of scrambled eggs, and so forth. This works. Young people take pride in mastering some dish. The technique can even work with chores. I had a Refrigerator Knight whose job it was to chase down and slay all the green dragons that grew in the produce drawers during the week.

Broccoli Frittata

The frittata is Italy's answer to the omelet. It's the coward's answer, too, because a French omelet makes home cooks nervous. They've heard it requires a special seasoned pan that is not to be used for anything but omelets. (This is a hilarious notion to anyone experienced in the family pots-and-pans department.) Home cooks are also afraid they'll rip the darn thing and all the filling will leak out.

So relax and make this frittata instead. It's an easy, low-risk and delicous way to sneak a vegetable into the family diet. This particular recipe is for broccoli and is an effective way to make the green bits palatable to those who usually avoid them.

In removing some of the fat from the traditional recipe, I've cut back on the egg yolks and bacon. If you need to stay away from egg yolks, cheese and bacon entirely, the whole dish can be made with six egg whites—minus the bacon and cheese.

1 tablespoon olive oil	2 whole eggs *plus* 4 egg whites
1 cup onion, chopped	Salt and pepper
2 cups fresh or frozen broccoli bits, chopped	2 slices Canadian bacon, chopped
2 garlic cloves, minced	1/2 cup grated Parmesan cheese
2 teaspoons fresh basil (or 1 teaspoon dried)	

Heat the broiler.

In a large flameproof skillet, heat the oil and sauté the onions over medium-high for about 5 minutes. Add the broccoli bits, garlic and basil, cooking and stirring another 5 minutes.

Then, in a large bowl, beat the eggs and egg whites with a fork or whip until a slight froth appears on the top. Salt and pepper the egg mixture.

Add the bacon to the hot pan. Add the eggs, lifting and turning the pan so the eggs flow all over the surface and between the broccoli bits.

Turn the heat to low and cook, covered, for 3 or 4 minutes, or until the eggs become firmer.

(*Continued*)

Then remove the cover and top with the Parmesan cheese. Put the skillet under the hot broiler until the cheese begins to brown. Don't leave broiler watch.

Warning

Don't top with nonfat cheese. Nonfat cheese melts best at low temperatures: This dish is finished under a hot broiler.

Cut the frittata in half or quarters. It is cut and served much more easily when slightly cooled. Freshly toasted herb bread, juicy sliced tomatoes and a mixed baby-lettuce salad would be excellent companions.

As a main dish, serves 4 people who hate broccoli or 2 who love it.

Baked Cheese-and-Tomato Sandwiches

This is supper for the nights when terminal fatigue has set in. You're too tired to go out for fast food and too hungry to wait for the pizza-delivery boy.

First, lift your weary hand and turn the oven to 325°. Then assemble:

4 slices French bread
Dijon mustard and mayonnaise to spread on the bread

1 large (or 2 small) tomatoes, sliced
2/3 cup grated cheese (cheddar, Monterey Jack—whatever's in the house)

Lay the bread on a greased baking sheet. Cover with the mustard/mayo combo. Top with tomato slices. Sprinkle with cheese. Bake 15 minutes, or until cheese is melted and bread is brown at edges.

You can hold your head up with this recipe because it is very good. Made with in-season tomatoes, interesting mustard and excellent bread, it is out of this world.

A green salad is nice if you have the energy to put it together.

Serves 2 starving people or 4 who ate a late lunch.

Learn to Love Your Microwave

Guerrilla Strategy

Riding the 'Wave

Some are born to the microwave, but others have the microwave thrust upon them.

Many people have to be forced to meet and use their microwaves. Face it. A microwave has as much visual charisma as a VCR. Besides, we guerrillas don't want to meet anything that has an instruction booklet.

People are sucked into microwaving by moving into a house that has a microwave. Or maybe they're given the appliance for Christmas by a gadget-loving husband. My friend Joan found a microwave under the tree and hoped it was for somebody else. The dog, maybe. But alas, she was the only cook in the house. She was so upset that she went into a closet and wept.

Do not cry. The microwave can be one of your best kitchen buddies. The clue to falling deeply and truly in love with your microwave is this: Don't have unrealistic expectations about the relationship.

Your microwave is not a regular oven or a cooktop or a barbecue. It won't brown things or bake well. But learn just a few new tricks and the microwave will help you get out of the kitchen and on with your life.

Many of the recipes in this book suggest speed-cooking in a microwave rather than cooking more slowly on a stovetop. Unless otherwise noted, all recipes are cooked at full power for an average 800-watt microwave.

The Many Talents of Your Microwave

The microwave has a way with vegetables, turning out crisp and colorful dishes that retain vitamins and essential taste. It does not reduce vegetables to undifferentiated gray shapes. A microwaved vegetable is a happy vegetable. As for the big veggies, the microwave can take care of an entire eggplant in just 9 minutes.

Baked fruit is a natural for this appliance. Many a hunger emergency can be addressed by a quickly baked apple or warm and creamy bananas.

On the breakfast front, bacon is ready in a few minutes and doesn't have to be watched or baby-sat in a skillet.

Of course, the microwave rewarms coffee and tea.

At dinnertime, the microwave will transform fish into a cooked but still-moist entrée, without frying otherwise upping the fat grams. And if you are not cooking that night, the microwave rewarms leftovers without burning or drying the food.

The microwave can help bring up baby. Just cook the food in the microwave, remove it and run it through the blender. Then reheat the puree in the microwave, but be sure to stir and taste the results for temperature.

As for miscellaneous virtues, sauces are a snap in the microwave. (Check out the instant sauces and toppings in the dessert chapter.) Even nuts can be warmed as an appetizer or quickly browned as a topping. Store-bought cookies microwaved for 15 seconds will feel warm and home-made. Need to melt butter or chocolate? Do it in seconds in the microwave. Need to start a dish by cooking chopped onions in butter or oil? Do it in the "wave." Even ice cream that's too hard to serve can be microwaved for 15 seconds or so to soften it.

And did you go off to work and forget to defrost the chicken or hamburger for dinner? Not to worry. The microwave is your slave when it comes to quick defrosting. And are you starving for lunch or a snack but don't want to cook for real? Micro-bake a sweet potato or a hunk of squash and serve it slathered in salsa and nonfat sour cream.

As for baked white potatoes, I confess I prefer the oven-baked to those from the microwave; but when I'm in a hurry, I'll run baking potatoes in the microwave for five minutes—until I can smell them—and then finish them in a 400° oven to get the crispiness on the skin. You can't tell them from the oven-baked.

So Why Don't Microwaves Get More Respect?

People who cook professionally set the trends, and they tend not to rely heavily on microwaves for the heart of their cooking. Microwaves won't handle large volumes of food. Besides, the tradition in the professional culinary world is based on cooktops and ovens. For instance, just think of the cooking shows on TV—it's a chef with a cooktop and an oven, not a chef with a microwave.

Microwaving Hints

Don't go freestyle when it comes to following the cooking times suggested in a recipe. Microwaves are powerful and can overcook very quickly. As noted before, the recipes in this book were tested in an 800-watt microwave used at regular high power. Less-powerful microwaves will require a little more time for cooking.

➡ Get a carousel microwave or a turning device to go in an uncarouseled microwave. They save work—you don't have to turn the food—and they make the food cook more evenly.

➡ Don't use metal or dishes with metallic trim.

➡ Do use pot holders and remove any hot plastic wrapping carefully. Double-check temperatures when serving infants and little people.

➡ Pyrex is wonderful as a microwavable cook-and-serve material. So is the entire French family of white ceramics: ramekins, soufflé and au gratin dishes. (Ramekins look like little soufflé dishes that never grew up. They're great for baking fruit and melting butter.)

➡ To minimize exposure to the minirays, don't stand with your face in the viewing door watching something cook. Remember, though, experts say that a microwave has less radiation than a TV set.

➡ A microwave uses far less power than conventional ovens and will cut utility bills.

➡ A microwave saves dishwashing. Serve right out of the cooking dish.

➡ A microwave is cool on summer nights. No slaving over a hot stove.

➡ A microwave makes a good bread box when it's not in use.

3 Forging Appetizers:
Quick and Sneaky Starters

APPETIZERS: OR, STAY AWAY FROM THE PORK TARTARE

Appetizers: Or, Stay Away from the Pork Tartare

Most days, an appetizer is what the cook snitches from the pot while making dinner. Piece o' pasta—the house hors d'oeuvre.

During the workweek, few of us can rouse ourselves to plan, cook and clean up after an appetizer unless guests are on the premises. Even then, hosts and hostesses are reluctant to fool with a serious beginning because it means more work.

Someone giving a dinner party may already have figured out a special dinner menu, done the food shopping, worked up the main course and the things that go with it, cleaned the house, set the table, made a centerpiece, told the kids to pick up their toys, picked up the kids' toys, forgot all about dessert but then settled on ice cream and finally dragged off to try and find something in the closet that still fits.

And this person is supposed to think of appetizers?

So appetizers had better be mostly easy, though one or two lollapaloozas are nice to have on hand for state occasions, major celebrations and unanticipated fits of domesticity.

Appetizers should be light. They should not compete with dinner. I say this because it is a good way to get out of cooking elaborate appetizers: the molded gelatin rings, the frozen-puff-pastry dealies and the itsy-bitsy sandwiches with the crusts cut off.

Anyhow, it is also *true* that you shouldn't serve a lot of food before dinner. You really don't want to spoil the assembled appetites. So this is what you say if you are caught with your canapés down:

"I just hated to spoil your dinner."

Nothing at All

Among the best chefs I know are a married couple who are inspired professional cooks. They sometimes serve no appetizer at all when cooking at home for neighbors and friends. Wine, yes; hors d'oeuvres, no. They don't want to spoil dinner, and when dinner comes, you are glad they didn't.

The nothing-at-all strategy works only if dinner is at an early hour and appears on the table shortly after your guests' arrival. On the other hand, you should offer an appetizer if dinner is at a late hour, if the predinner drinking is likely to be long and enthusiastic, or if guests have come a long way to get to your house. Also, if you or anybody else is just plain starving, the jig is up on the idea of nothing at all. You must respond with a quick guerrilla appetizer.

Micro-Cooked Grapes

1 large grape cluster

Warmed clusters of grapes make great pre-dinner grazing. Think of this appetizer before an intimate two-person dinner. Just put a cluster of fresh, firm grapes in the microwave for 1 minute. Then, seated by the fire, eat them off the stems, one by one. Warming brings out their fragrance. Grapes are also good dipped into whipped herb cheeses such as Boursin.

Now, purists would tell you to eat fruit after dinner, not before, but all's fair in love and cooking. Besides, it is difficult to eat the five recommended servings of fruits and vegetables every day. So use any quick idea that gets the good stuff into your eating audience, no matter what others say.

One cluster serves 2.

More pre-dinner fruit ideas:

➡ Small wedges of watermelon dipped in cold tequila

➡ Cantaloupe wedges, either plain or wrapped in thin prosciutto

➡ Fresh cherries with a tray of cream cheese and crackers

➡ Pears along with a wedge of ripe Camembert

➡ Apples next to a round of Gouda cheese

Warm Nuts and Hot Pretzels

For emergencies, put mixed nuts and pretzel sticks in your pantry. The nuts satisfy the seriously starving; the pretzels please those looking for lower-fat cocktail fodder. Put each food in a bowl and run one bowl at a time in the microwave until warm. About 45 seconds will do for the pretzels. They burn easily. The nuts will take at least 60 seconds. A 300° oven will accomplish the same thing for both but will take 15 minutes.

Those famous goldfish crackers now come in pretzel form, which gives fans of the cracker fish a lower-fat alternative.

One large soup bowl of cocktail fodder serves 3–4.

Cucumber Rounds and Red Pepper Strips

2 cucumbers, sliced
4 red peppers, seeded and cut into strips

The Dip
1/2 cup nonfat sour cream

1/2 cup light mayonnaise
**2 teaspoons chopped fresh tarragon
(or 1 teaspoon dried tarragon)**
Salt and lemon pepper to taste

To fancy up the cucumber rounds, take a fork and, using hard pressure, run the tines down the sides of the cucumbers. You are making a decorative pattern, raking the skin away and revealing the white cucumber underneath. Slice into rounds, which will now have serrated edges. Arrange them nicely on a serving plate.

Halve and seed the peppers. Cut them into strips, adding to the serving dish.

Mix the sour cream, mayonnaise, tarragon, salt and lemon pepper. Serve in a dipping bowl with plenty of napkins.

If you have a jar of refrigerated pickles on hand, add a little pickle juice to this dip for a hint of dill and vinegar.

Serves 6.

Vodka Tomatoes

This appetizer fascinates guests because it is not an everyday kind of food experience. Specifically, the eater's job is to pick up a cherry tomato by its green stem, dip the tomato in a saucer of cold vodka, then dip it in a saucer of seasoned salt and pop it in the mouth. This is a great icebreaker as people sit around dipping and popping.

2 pint baskets cherry tomatoes (red and yellow, if possible)

1 saucer cold vodka

1 saucer seasoned salt (found in the spice section of the market)

Visually, the tomatoes look nice in a wicker basket. Decorative saucers for the vodka and salt make this display even more special.

Serves 6.

Melted Cheese and Crackers

¹/₂ pound cheese (Brie, cheddar or Monterey Jack)

2 cups crackers (melba toast, crisp thins or sesame rounds)

Warm cheese on hot crackers is a comfort food. Just put a ¹/₂-pound slab of cheese such as Brie, cheddar or Monterey Jack in the microwave for about 1 minute, or until the sides begin to melt.

Next, micro-cook a bowl of crackers for about 30 seconds. Spread the cheese on the crackers. If you like, rerun the cheese in the microwave when the cheese gets cold again. As the hunk of cheese gets smaller, having been attacked by hungry eaters, micro-cook only 30 seconds.

If your idea of heaven is a cheese so melted that it looks like fondue, make sure the container has sides to hold in the spread. Micro-cook in 30-second increments until the melt is satisfactory.

Of course, you can also use the oven at 300° to warm up the cheese and crackers, but it will take 15 minutes.

Serves 4.

Whipped Herb Cheese on Lettuce Tips (Two Quick Versions)

Whipped herb cheese now comes in a lighter style with 50 percent less fat. Here are two recipes using it. Both involve serving individual lettuce leaves decorated with a cheese payload.

Version #1 has three ingredients, though you can go for the fancy shrimped-up version #2, which has five.

Version #1

6¹/₂-ounce container of whipped herb-and-garlic cheese

1 head romaine (or 1 head of endive)
Parsley (for garnish)

Take the small inner leaves of a head of romaine lettuce (or endive). Fan them out gracefully on a serving dish. At the bottom or root end of each leaf, spread a bit of the cheese. If you have the time and spirit, garnish the cheese with parsley bits.

Version #2

Add to the recipe above:
Dabs of light mayonnaise

¹/₂ pound small cooked shrimp

Take the inner romaine leaves or a head of endive and fan the leaves out on a serving plate. Spread a bit of the herbed cheese on the bottom or root end of each leaf. Dab on a bit of light mayo. Place a small shrimp on top of each mayo dab. Garnish the shrimp with a bit of parsley.

Each version serves 4.

An Oven-Baked Trio

Mushrooms, olives and garlic—these can bake as you shower and get dressed for a company dinner. Each ingredient has its own easy recipe, and each is served in its own dish. You can, of course, use just one of the following three recipes, but it is smart to run the oven once and yet get three different dishes when you open the oven door. Also smart: doing something relaxing out of the kitchen while the food cooks unattended.

Start with—

Marsala Mushrooms

This is an extra-easy, extra-special roast veggie. The mushrooms are baked in marsala, a common and inexpensive wine that lends a sweet—but not cloying—taste.

1 pound fresh mushrooms, washed
3/4 cup marsala wine

Salt and pepper to taste
2 tablespoons fresh parsley, chopped

Heat the oven to 350°.

Place the mushrooms, stem side up, in a greased baking/serving dish. Pour marsala wine on and around the mushrooms. Let them bake 1 hour, basting once or twice. The caramelizing wine—all brown and sweet—gives the mushrooms wonderful flavor, fragrance and taste. When done, sprinkle with salt, pepper and freshly chopped parsley.

People will pick up the mushrooms by their stems. Have napkins at the ready.

This is also a great side dish for dinner.

Serves 6.

Roasted Black Olives

Oven-roasted black olives are unusual, easy, delicious and wonderfully fragrant, a good culinary investment of your time. The baking brings the olive flavor to a bravura level of performance. The dish is so simple, it's almost embarrassing to have guests "oh" and "ah" while you sit there knowing it took little effort and that a chimp could do it.

This simple beginning wins consistent first-place votes within my eating pack. People love the surprise of the temperature. What is usually cold is now hot. Neat!

10-ounce jar plump Kalamata (or other good black olives)
1 tablespoon olive oil
1 teaspoon grated lemon peel

Garnish
Thin slices of lemon peel and freshly chopped parsley

Heat the oven to 350°.

Drain the olive brine down the sink as an offering to the garbage-disposal gods. Rinse off the extra salt from the olives and then dump them, single-layer, into a baking dish. Add the olive oil and lemon peel. Mix gently so that the olives are coated in oil. Bake in a 350° oven for 45 minutes, though they can bake 1 hour or more. Sometimes the brine rises to the surface of the olive during baking. Don't worry. Just roll the olives around in the dish, and the little salt spots will disappear.

Present with thin lemon slices and scattered fresh parsley.

This dish may be prepared with canned pitted black olives, but palates that have been around the block will prefer the Kalamata olives.

Serves 4.

Mellow Garlic Spread

Work magic in the kitchen. Take a fiery head of garlic and tame it into a sweet and mild paste to spread on the edible surface of your choice. Toasted baguette rounds would be nice. Each of your guests will get a whole *head* of garlic and will love it.

For *each* person, you will need:

1 whole head garlic   **1 teaspoon olive oil**
1 custard cup (or small baking ramekin)

Whack off the top third of each garlic head with a knife. If you don't know where the head of a head of garlic is, just aim for the pointy side opposite the vestigial root.

Put a little olive oil in the bottom of each cup. Stick the head of garlic in the cup with the cut side down. Bake for 1 hour at 350°. The temperature and timing aren't critical. Garlic heads can cook longer, and they just get softer and sweeter.

Serve each person his or her own custard cup of garlic. Put thinly sliced and toasted bread in the middle of the table. The idea is for each person to squeeze out the garlic from the head and spread it on the bread. The other idea is for you *not* to do it for them: Guerrillas delegate.

This is a good appetizer if you're sitting outdoors looking for something to do while the chicken barbecues. Served with the baked mushrooms and baked olives from the recipes above, it is almost a feast in itself.

Each garlic head serves 1.
Really.

Crispy Eggplant Rounds

1 eggplant, sliced into ¼" rounds (no thicker)

½ cup light mayonnaise
1 cup Parmesan cheese, grated

Slice the eggplant into rounds, leaving the skin on. Lay out the rounds on two sprayed or oiled baking sheets. If the rounds are too large in diameter to be manageable as finger food, cut them in half. Spread each piece with a thin layer of light mayo. Sprinkle on the Parmesan cheese. Bake at 400° for 20 minutes, or until the cheese begins to brown a little.

These are best when eaten promptly.

Makes about 18 rounds or enough for 3–4 people.

Sesame Chicken Strips

Use these as an appetizer for a light meal, or even as the main course. Sesame Chicken Strips are easy, delicious and feature a guerrilla cook's secret weapon: hoisin sauce. Hoisin sauce can be found in the Asian food section of your supermarket. It's wonderful to dab on pork roasts, duck and chicken.

1 pound skinless, boneless chicken breasts
3 tablespoons hoisin sauce
1 tablespoon apple cider vinegar

1 teaspoon garlic, minced
1 tablespoon sesame seeds, toasted

Cut the chicken into strips about ¼" wide. Thread the strips onto skewers. Combine the hoisin, vinegar and garlic and brush on the chicken strips. Toast the sesame seeds about 1 minute in the microwave and then sprinkle over the chicken.

Grill the strips on the barbecue or broil them on each side about 3 minutes, or until done. *(Continued)*

Forging Appetizers: Quick and Sneaky Starters

Watch, because they cook fast.

If you are using bamboo skewers, soak them in water before using so they're less likely to burn.

Serves 4.

Shrimp Quesadillas

8" flour tortilla
2 heaping tablespoons part-skim moz-
   zarrella cheese, shredded

2 tablespoons mild green taco sauce
Scant 1/4 cup small cooked shrimp

Put a tortilla on a microwave-safe plate, topping it with cheese, then taco sauce and the shrimp. (Cooked sausage or ham bits can be used instead of shrimp.)

Cook in the microwave for 60 seconds.

Oven alternative: You can warm several prepared tortillas in a preheated oven for about 10 minutes at 375°, or until the cheese is melted.

To devour efficiently, roll up the tortilla.

This fast, microwavable recipe serves 1. Multiply as appropriate. With a salad and 2 quesadillas per person, you can even call it dinner.

Garden Sticks and Shards

The smart approach to the traditional vegetable basket is to use vegetables that don't take lots of peeling, chopping or other active participation. So think about snow peas and cherry tomatoes. Even think baby asparagus. Young asparagus can bring fresh life to the appetizer tray. Eaters will applaud, especially if you provide a good dip.

As for other vegetable ideas, zucchini and cucumbers are easy to slice and don't have to be peeled, though waxed cukes are appealing only to people who ate their crayons as kids.

Fresh steamed string beans are great. Broccoli and cauliflower can be whacked off their stems and pulled into edible bits in a minute or two. They are improved by a quick round in the microwave—say, 2 minutes—to get their rawness toned down.

Broccoli and cauliflower also leave lots of cruciferous crumbles on the counter. So place your cutting board on a piece of newspaper. Then just scrumple up the stray bits in the paper and toss.

For a special presentation, line a wicker basket with plastic wrap and then add a colorful napkin or checkered dish towel. Pile the vegetables about artistically. Use a basket with a big overhead handle—the kind a romantic heroine would use for gathering roses.

Serves as many as you like, depending on your capacity for peeling and chopping. If you overdo on the amount, use the leftovers for a stir-fry or in a soup.

Hot Veggie Bits

Here's another idea for your bag of tricks: a role-reversal recipe that's easy and good. Vegetable trays are usually served cold at the cocktail hour. But raw broccoli does not often warm the heart, whatever it may do to save it.

So you know what you are going to do here.

Yes, serve the cold stuff hot. This appetizer will give a good start to a cold-weather meal of roasted meat, a hefty salad of winter greens and warm bread.

14¹/₂-ounce can chicken broth
1 tablespoon olive oil
Freshly ground pepper
2 cups carrot chunks

2 cups zucchini rounds
2 cups assorted sweet peppers, seeded and cut into chunks
Salt to taste

Heat the oven to 350°.

The idea is to roast bite-sized bits of carrots in the oven, along with zucchini chunks and hunks of variously colored peppers. I keep each vegetable in a separate section on the baking pan, but you can mix them together, if you prefer.

The vegetables are baked in chicken broth with a bit of olive oil to keep them moist. Use a baking pan or cookie sheet with sides high enough to hold the broth and oil.

First add the broth, the oil and the freshly ground pepper to the roasting pan. Then add the vegetables and bake 1 hour. Baste once or twice. Put your feet up. The guerrilla appetizers are making themselves. Salt to taste when finished. Large-grained sea salt is good if you have it on hand.

Serve warm or at room temperature with toothpicks and napkins, though guests have been known to forget the niceties and attack barehanded. Use leftover vegetables at the next dinner, draped fetchingly over pasta.

For a slightly fancier presentation, try a little grated ginger over the carrots, a little oregano on the zucchini, a little Parmesan on the peppers.

Serves 8.

Faux Stuffed Eggs

People shy away from stuffed eggs, expecting to expire on the spot from eating egg yolks. Too bad, because stuffed eggs are a longtime American favorite. To update the recipe and soothe the cholesterol-concerned, I stuff the eggs with soy-based "egg" salad, which may be found in either a health-food store or the health-food section of your supermarket. If you can't find this ingredient—it comes in a refrigerated plastic tub—simply use fresh store-bought salsa, drained, as a stuffing.

8 eggs, hard-boiled
2 8-ounce containers soy-based "egg" salad

Garnish
Freshly chopped parsley

Put the eggs in a saucepan filled with water. Bring the eggs to a boil and then simmer at least 12 minutes, or until hard-boiled. When cool enough to handle, shell the eggs and cut in half lengthwise. Scoop out the yolks and discard. Fill with the tofu "egg" salad or with well-drained fresh salsa. Garnish with freshly chopped parsley. To brighten up the tofu salad, add small bits of parsley to that, too.

Use your imagination about other stuffings. Sardine lovers can mash and stuff the eggs with sardines packed in mustard or tomato sauce. Try tuna salad with capers or use the Indian Carrot Spread in this chapter.

Serves 6–8.

Baked Bread and Brie

This old favorite never fails to disappear. After the dish is prepared, it needs no tending, only baking. This is not low-fat, so save it for special occasions.

1 round French bread, unsliced
2 wedges Brie cheese (about 1½ pounds)

1 baguette French bread, cut into rounds

(Continued)

Heat the oven to 375°.

Take the bread round and cut horizontally, completely across the top of the loaf. Make the cut about one-third of the way down. Remove the top of the loaf. Scoop out the bread inside the loaf, leaving the outside crust intact. Reserve the loaf top and bread chunks for later cheese-dipping.

Break the cheese into pieces and stuff the loaf with them. Don't pile them over the top of the loaf. Wrap the loaf in one layer of aluminum foil and bake for 1 hour, or until the cheese is completely melted.

During the last 10 minutes of baking, put the sliced baguette rounds plus the bread chunks and the loaf top on a baking sheet in the oven to warm.

When the hour is up or the cheese is melted, remove the wrapped loaf and warmed bread. Remove the foil from the loaf.

To present, put the loaf in the middle of a serving dish. Place the warmed baguette rounds and loaf top around the cheese-stuffed loaf. Dip the bread in the cheese or use knives as a spreader. Typically, people do both. Encourage guests to break up the loaf top into edible pieces and devour.

Serves 6–8.

The Dip Eternal

Dips are the classic appetizer of our culture. No matter how many fancy-pants alternatives we see in magazines and books, no matter what we order in restaurants, at home we love dips. They are easy. It's dump the chips in a basket, dump the dip in a bowl and then eat. Dips don't have to be cooked, timed, or piped through pastry bags. They can be done ahead. They are comradely and communal, one of the few dishes we share. It's *everybody* into the dip, which is, of course, a smart strategy—preparation by proxy, getting someone else to put the appetizer payload on the carrying surface of chips or vegetables.

Fresh Onion Dip

In the old days, long before Americans discovered arugula, onion dip was the star of the home cocktail circuit. It was made with salt-laden soup mix and fatty sour cream, and so fell into disfavor. But, darn, it was good and very easy, which was why every hostess between Providence and Portland knew and used the recipe.

To renovate this dish, I've come up with a dip made with fresh onions and nonfat sour cream. I think it's just as addictive as the older version.

It's also fabulous over baked potatoes.

1 onion, finely chopped	**1 tablespoon light mayonnaise**
2 teaspoons olive oil	**Salt and pepper to taste**
1 cup nonfat sour cream	**Milk to thin (optional)**

Peel the onion and chop finely. Put in a microwavable dish with the olive oil. Make sure the dish is big enough to accommodate a single layer of onions. Stir to coat all the onions. Microwave 4 minutes. Stir. Run another 4 minutes, or until the onions are mostly brown but not burned.

Stovetop alternative

You can sauté the onions in oil over medium-high heat until they are crisp but not burned. Use a nonstick pan for easy cleanup. If your microwave doesn't have a turning carousel, cook the onions on the stovetop. It's easier. *(Continued)*

However you cook the onions, add them to the sour cream and mayo. Add salt and pepper to taste. Thin with a few teaspoons of milk if you wish.

Store covered in the refrigerator.

Present with chips or vegetables. Red, green and yellow sweet peppers would be good.

Note
The onion bits in the dip are most crisp when the dip is freshly made.

Serves 4.

Five-Layer Dip

This is a favorite of all ages, genders and degrees of culinary sophistication. It is good, fast, foolproof and a great opener for a fiesta kind of dinner. It disappears very fast at any browsing event where people think they can get away with repeated visits to the same dish without being observed.

Game plan: You are going to layer different dips in one serving dish, preferably a clear-glass, straight-sided dish so people can see the wondrously colored substrata of culinary geology.

This dish is invincible for a general audience, with the following warning: Do not layer the food so deeply that people cannot get their chips to the bottom without plunging in up to their wrists.

2 15-ounce cans refried beans (without lard)

2 ripe avocados

16-ounce tub nonfat sour cream

4-ounce can chopped green chiles

15-ounce tub fresh-made salsa (from the dairy case)

Dipping chips (tortilla chips or blue corn chips)

Leave out the avocados if you're going low-cal this week, and don't put them on top, or the air will turn them brown.

Layer the beans on the bottom. Then, one by one, layer the chiles, salsa and avocado. Put the sour cream on top as "frosting." Garnish with something lively. Bright orange nasturtiums would be perfect.

Serves 10–12.

Spinach Dip

There are several versions of the American culinary set piece, the spinach dip. This one is fast and less caloric than most. It's best made a day ahead, so the flavors blend. It is very thick—more a spread than a dip—and full of good green things. Leftovers, if any, make a fine topping for baked potatoes.

10-ounce package chopped spinach (cooked and well-drained)
¹/₂ cup fresh parsley, finely chopped
¹/₂ cup green onions, finely chopped
1 cup nonfat sour cream

¹/₄ cup light mayonnaise
1 teaspoon garlic salt
1 teaspoon dill (dried)
Salt to taste

Cook the spinach according to package directions. Drain well. Cool and wring out the excess water. Mix the spinach with all the other ingredients. Taste and then add more salt if needed. Cover and refrigerate. Spread on crackers, toasted baguette rounds or slices of cucumber.

Serves 8.

Caper Cream

Soybean products such as tofu are highly regarded by nutritionists and environmentalists. They provide low-cost protein at low cost to the environment. The more tofu you eat, the more you are saving the earth by eating lower on the food chain.

1/2 **pound soft tofu**
1 cup nonfat sour cream
2 cloves garlic
**1 tablespoon cooking oil (canola or saf-
flower)**

2 tablespoons capers
2 tablespoons caper juice
**A green garnish (fresh parsley, chives,
whatever)**

Mix all the ingredients except the garnish in the blender. Stop and scrape down the sides to make sure all gets mixed. Place in serving bowl. Garnish.

That's it. Use carrots or colorful pepper strips as dippers.

Serves 4.

Aztec Dip

This dip takes just a few minutes to mix together and keeps for days.

15-ounce tub fresh salsa
**17-ounce can corn, drained (or 2 fresh
ears, cooked)**
15-ounce can kidney beans, drained
1 onion, finely chopped
1 tablespoon chili powder

1 tablespoon parsley, chopped
1 tablespoon cilantro, chopped
2 pinches sugar

Garnish
Cilantro (optional)

Chop the onions. Place them in a microwavable dish and cook them in the microwave for 5 minutes. Dump them in a bowl with all the other ingredients. Mix.

Serve with blue-corn tortilla chips or any good baked chips. You can also spoon this hearty salsa into the small inside leaves of a head of romaine. Reheat any leftover dip as a side vegetable dish.

If you want to take more trouble, instead of the canned corn, use fresh corn scraped from two husked cobs that have been wrapped in plastic and cooked in the microwave for 4 minutes.

Garnish with cilantro if you like.

Serves 10–12.

Mockamole

Mockamole is a great grazing item for dieters. It does a good imitation of guacamole without the avocado fat. My test eaters give this recipe high marks. Vary the hot pepper and garlic to your taste.

1 pound frozen asparagus, steamed
3 teaspoons fresh lemon juice
4 tablespoons onion, chopped
1 cup fresh tomato, finely diced
1 teaspoon salt

$1/4$ teaspoon chili powder
$1/2$ teaspoon garlic, minced
$1/8$ teaspoon cayenne pepper (or 2–3 dashes hot pepper sauce)
4 tablespoons nonfat sour cream

Steam the asparagus until lightly cooked but still green. Mix with the rest of the ingredients in a blender. Blend just until mixed. Stop and scrape down the sides if necessary. Refrigerate for at least 2–3 hours. (Cover first with plastic wrap that sits right on the surface of the dip. This prevents air from discoloring the ingredients.)

Mockamole is good as a dip for vegetables—try cold cucumber rounds—or use nonfat tortilla chips as scoops.

Serves 6.

Roquefort Mold

This used to be a fussy recipe for a molded hors d'oeuvre, but it has undergone guerrilla modification into an appetizer that takes just 8 minutes to prepare.

Notice that there is no risky unmolding of the gelatin, no holding the dish under hot water, no inverting on slippery platters, no knifing, no pounding on the mold to let go. Just serve this appetizer right in the mold. Scoop it out and spread on a cracker.

1/4 cup cold water	6 ounces nonfat cream cheese
1 tablespoon unflavored gelatin	6 ounces Roquefort (or other blue cheese)
1/2 cup nonfat milk	
1/2 teaspoon Worcestershire sauce	2 tablespoons chopped green onions

Put the water in a small saucepan. Add the gelatin. Let the mixture stand for a few minutes. Then place over low heat to dissolve the gelatin. When the liquid looks clear, remove from the heat and cool.

In a blender, put the gelatin/water mix, milk, Worcestershire sauce and cream cheese. Blend and then add the Roquefort and onions. (Stop at least once and scrape the sides down with a spatula so all the goods get mixed in.)

Place in a pretty mold. I use a flat tart pan. Garnish in a sprightly manner. Keep refrigerated until served. Serve with little bread rounds or good crackers.

For party use, this can be made as much as 2 days ahead and either served as is or stuffed into celery for an appetizer. Get someone else to stuff the celery. Put paprika on top for the visual hit of red.

Serves 6.

Shrimp Toast

Oh, how the shrimp toast of yesterday used to swim in fat.

Here is an updated version, one that *broils* the toast and comes with a surprise topping of fluffy, toasted egg whites—a cocktail meringue, if you will. This dish can be made in 10 minutes.

1 pound shrimp, cooked and cleaned (not canned)	**Salt**
2 tablespoons light mayonnaise	**Optional Garnish**
1 baguette, sliced	**Dill, freshly chopped**
2 egg whites	

Heat the broiler.

Chop the shrimp into a semi-paste. They will be easier to chop if they are half-frozen. Add mayonnaise and spread on rounds of sliced French bread.

Whip the egg whites into peaks. That should take 45 seconds with a hand mixer. Add a bit of salt to the whites. Spread the whites on top of the shrimp toast. The meringue should not be piled too high because you want the egg white to cook all the way through under the broiler.

Broil until light brown and toasty, about 3 minutes on the lowest shelf. Do not leave broiler watch—this happens very fast.

A few bits of dill for garnish would be nice.

This dish can be partly prepared ahead for guests. Chop the shrimp, slice the bread, even whip the egg whites. Whipped egg whites will stay usable in the refrigerator for at least 4 hours. At the last minute, put the shrimp on the bread, the egg white on the shrimp and the whole shebang under the broiler.

Makes about 16 pieces.

New Presentations

Sometimes we get sick of the same-old, same-old and look for new tastes or new ways of presenting favorite old tastes. Here are a few ideas.

Indian Carrot Spread

An unusual and delicious spread, this one is served at room temperature. It can also be served warm as a thoroughly different side dish for dinner.

2¹/₂ cups carrots, grated (about 5 large carrots)

1 tablespoon butter (or cooking oil)

2 green onions, chopped

1 clove garlic, minced

1 teaspoon fennel seeds

¹/₄ teaspoon ground cumin

¹/₈ teaspoon ground red pepper

¹/₂ teaspoon salt

Grate the carrots, using the big holes on the grater.

In a large saucepan, melt the butter (or warm the oil). Add the remaining ingredients, except for the carrots. Cook for 1 or 2 minutes over medium heat. Add the carrots. Cover and stir for 4 or 5 minutes. Remove from heat. Mash the contents around a bit. Serve with sesame crackers.

This recipe makes for a good lunch the day after. Roll the spread in a lettuce leaf as a veggie burrito.

Serves 6–8.

Mushroom Spread

This is elegant but easy—a good party dish because it can be made ahead. The ingredient list is longer than most guerrilla recipes, but this recipe is fast to make.

1/2 cup walnuts, chopped

2 tablespoons butter

1/4 cup shallots, chopped

1/2 pound mushrooms, chopped

3 ounces nonfat cream cheese

1/2 teaspoon dried thyme (or 1 teaspoon fresh thyme, chopped)

2 tablespoons parsley, chopped

1/2 teaspoon salt

1/8 teaspoon ground red pepper

1 tablespoon sherry (optional but good)

Garnish

Chopped parsley and chopped walnuts

In the microwave, cook the walnuts in a single layer, uncovered, until toasted—about 2 minutes. Or you can toast the nuts on a baking sheet for 10–12 minutes in a 325° oven.

Next, in a large frying pan, melt the butter and add the chopped shallots. Stir and cook a few minutes over medium heat until soft but not browned. Add the mushrooms and cook until they are soft, about 7 minutes.

Then, in a blender or food processor, combine all the ingredients. If desired, add the optional sherry. Process until ingredients are finely minced.

Cover the finished spread and keep as long as 2 days. Let it soften to room temperature before serving. If the spread is in a microwavable serving dish, warm it in the microwave for 10 seconds to soften.

Top with chopped parsley and chopped walnuts. Present with toasted baguette rounds.

Serves 4–5.

Herbed Yogurt Cheese

It's easy to make "cheese" from store-bought nonfat yogurt. Just put the yogurt in a strainer or coffee filter and let the liquid drain out overnight in the refrigerator. Then use the resulting "cheese" as a spread.

Here's how to make a cheese yogurt flavored with enough herbs so that it has a little punch. People trying to avoid the fat in regular cheese go for this appetizer.

1 pound nonfat yogurt, unflavored, *without gelatin or stabilizers*

$1/4$ cup nonfat sour cream

3 tablespoons fresh herbs, chopped (see choices below)

3 cloves garlic, finely minced or pressed

1 tablespoon lemon juice

$1/8$ teaspoon cayenne pepper

Salt and lemon pepper to taste

Mix the ingredients together. Consider tarragon, basil, thyme, chives and/or dill as the herbs of choice. Use 1 tablespoon of dried herbs if you have no fresh ones at hand. My favorite combo is fresh basil and chives, along with pressed garlic.

To strain the herbed mixture, put it in a fine sieve suspended over a bowl that will catch the liquid. Try a paper coffee filter inside a large coffee cone or a colander lined with cheesecloth. (You can find cheesecloth in supermarkets, alongside the cooking utensils.) Whatever you use, make sure the strainer has a bowl under it to catch the liquid.

Leave your homemade contraption overnight in the refrigerator. In the morning, transfer the herb "cheese" to a serving dish. Spread on crisp, well-seasoned crackers.

Serves 4.

Garnishes: Dressing Up Dinner

Guerrilla Strategy

MEAT LOAF NEEDS MAKEUP

Garnish is makeup for food. If you do your face, you should do your food. You wouldn't get all gussied up and leave the house without doing your makeup. It's a small—but important—finishing touch. So, then, why put all that effort into cooking and just let the food lie there unadorned on the plate?

But that's not the way in our culture. It's American to sling the hash, un-American to garnish it. Only professionals are expected to doll up their dishes. We home cooks aren't taught much about dressing up dinner. A puff of parsley is max. This is strange because while Americans are taught the importance of looks in sexual appeal, we aren't taught how to use visual tactics to promote culinary arousal.

The fact is that people do eat first with their eyes. If a dish looks appetizing, the cook is halfway to success even before the first forkful. So smart cooks use quick tricks to make the food stand out visually. Garnishes are guerrilla.

Parsley

A few tablespoons of chopped garden-green parsley added to a dish or scattered over the top reinforces the idea of freshly made food. Parsley is wonderful on red and white foods. Flat-leaf Italian parsley is now replacing the curly variety on American tables. At the store, just make sure you don't grab cilantro instead of flat-leafed parsley. My grocery checker tells me that it happens all the time.

Cilantro

Frilly leafed cilantro is a pungent garnish, especially good with Mexican or Thai cooking. Unless you know your audience, a little goes a long way. You can chop and serve cilantro in a separate dish and let people decide for themselves. Again, don't confuse it with flat-leafed parsley. A sniff will tell you which is which.

Chives

Chives are a delicate cousin of the onion. Snip bits of chive all over the top of almost any savory dinner dish.

Watercress

Watercress tucked around meat or chicken on a serving plate is a visual pleasure as well as a taste treat. Watercress is good not only as a garnish, but as a filler for sandwiches. Use watercress leaves instead of lettuce, especially when a little extra burst of taste is needed, as in sliced roast beef sandwiches.

Mint

Mint sprigs can zip up lamb, iced drinks and poultry made with fruit sauces—chicken with apricots, duck with citrus, for instance. It's a great garnish for chocolate desserts or melon. Mint also can be used as a room freshener: A mint bouquet on the table adds a fresh and unexpected touch.

To Keep All These Herbs Fresh

Treat them like fresh flowers. Whack off the bottom of the bunch as soon as you get home from the store. Stick them in a vase or jar filled with water. Lemon and lime soda added to the water will keep them fresh—$2/3$ water, $1/3$ soda. The sugar and acid in the soda make the herbs last longer. Diet soda won't work.

Stick the container of herbs in the refrigerator with a plastic bag draped loosely over it. Clip from the herb bouquet as needed.

Nuts

Chopped or slivered nuts add texture and taste. Nuts pair naturally with vegetables: almonds on string beans, pecans on sweet potatoes, walnuts with eggplant, pine nuts with artichoke hearts. Cook the nuts for a minute or so in the microwave to warm them and bring out their flavor. My nut purveyor at the farmers' market says to freeze nuts if you're going to keep them more than a few weeks. Otherwise, they lose their freshness.

One guerrilla ploy is to use specially flavored nuts—you get two tastes from one product. Almonds come flavored with hickory smoke or honey. Slivered hickory-smoked almonds give a lift to creamy soups.

Seeds

Poppy seeds can liven up the tops of vegetable dishes. Sesame seeds may be toasted and scattered over rice.

Bacon

You can use the commercially made bits of bacon or keep Canadian bacon in the freezer. Cut the Canadian bacon with scissors, warm in the microwave or on the stovetop. Use the bits in salads, eggs, over potatoes, peas or on pizza.

Sour cream

Nonfat sour cream is evolving from okay to very good. If you've avoided sour cream because of the fat content, try again. Sour cream is great on Mexican food, fruit desserts and on the top of many pureed soups. It is extremely useful for appetizer dips.

Spices

When food needs dolling up, check out your spice shelf. Could that pale chicken breast use paprika? Do the carrots need a dash of nutmeg on top? Will the French toast look better with a shake of cinnamon? Obviously, the spice must complement the flavor of the food.

Ketchup

Ketchup? Yes, put some ketchup in a plastic squeeze bottle. Make patterns on the top of open-faced burgers. For kids especially, just serve the burger with the bun open and the meat decorated with ketchup pictures. Add their initials or a drawing of something simple—a mouse face, a sun. Let them try it themselves.

Another alternative for decorating: Stick some ketchup in the corner of a plastic sandwich bag, cut a tiny, tiny hole in that corner and use the bag as a decorating device—handling it as you would a cake-decorating bag. If you cut too big a hole, you'll lose control of your ketchup art.

So, garnishing means bang for the buck—a little effort for a big effect. Just a dollop, a leaf or a sprinkle makes your dish look finished and more delectable. About the only mistake you can make is overdoing it—decorating everything in sight. One or two garnished dishes are enough unless it's an elaborate buffet, in which case you probably were smart enough to hire a caterer to make the radish roses.

4 Desserts:
Or, Haven't I Cooked Enough Already?

WHIPPED CREAM IN YOUR DNA: WHY PEOPLE LOVE DESSERT

Whipped Cream in Your DNA: Why People Love Dessert

Chocolate lust is not your fault.

When we eat fattening sweets, we are merely obeying genetic instructions laid down long ago when our ancestors lived in caves and dined on greasy mammoth. As the human palate was forming, so the theory goes, our taste buds evolved in favor of fat. The cavewoman who chose calorically dense foods such as fat was the one most likely to survive when the food supply dwindled. She would have the body fat to burn, while a skinny leaf-eater was less likely to make it through the winter. Our fat ancestors lasted better than the thin ones, so the fat-loving genes of the survivors were the ones passed down to us. It's survival of the fattest.

But, today, with a stable food supply and easy access to fats, we and our genes tend to overdo it in the grease department. Fat is now hard to avoid. Unlike our ancestors, who had to hunt for their fat, all we have to do is call out for pizza.

Easy access to saturated fats means today's human can meet with unpleasant cardiac events and arterial jam-ups. Maybe we wouldn't have gotten into this biological mess if we were still out hunting and gathering; but here we are, unexercised, watching TV, eating ice cream and sitting on the couch listening to our fat cells expand.

Now food manufacturers have come out with a wide array of nonfat products. This should be a fine thing for all of us. However, instead of eating two cookies, people are eating the entire package. The sugar calories in the nonfat products add up, and so do the pounds.

Nonfat does not necessarily mean nonfattening.

Realism on the Dessert Table

So, yes, we should watch fat *and* total calories now that we're evolving into couch potatoes, but I have yet to meet anyone who doesn't like dessert. On the other hand, I have never met anyone who wishes to depart this earth earlier than necessary or go up a size. How to handle this dilemma was my question here: how to address the split between what we know we should eat for dessert—berries—and what our inner caveperson wants us to eat—butter cookies and whipped cream.

What I have assembled in this chapter is a range of choices to suit your every nutritional mood. There are healthy and high-flavor fruit desserts for your inner Jane Fonda, plus traditional dishes sensibly updated and defatted for those comfort cravings, as well as a few blowout recipes for the occasions when you or your Flintstone family want to spend a little quality time with butter and cream. Also included are some instant dips and sauces to gussy up ordinary desserts such as ice cream.

Here, too, you will discover the power of a splash of liqueur. When it comes to quick-and-easy flavor, liqueur is as useful to desserts as vanilla is to baking. So some of the desserts do use a splash of liqueur; but, whenever possible, I also indicate nonalcoholic alternatives.

Frozen Grapes

A dieter's dream, this is a great dessert snack to have on hand. No cooking here—just freezing. The taste? Like fresh grape sorbet.

1 or 2 clusters grapes (green, red or both)

Simply wash the grapes, pull them off the stems and put them in an uncovered bowl that will go into the freezer. Let them freeze. Then, anytime in the next few days that you want a dessert-type snack, go to the freezer and pry a few grapes out of the bowl.

These grapes are intriguingly frosty on the tongue—altogether a good substitute for the times when you crave sweets, but not the calories.

Serves 1.

Strawberries in Snow

Pay homage to the strawberry by dipping each piece gently into a snowy cream and nibbling the luscious result. Extra points if you use the large long-stemmed strawberries of spring. For a healthy dinner-party dessert, serve each guest a little plate of large strawberries and pass a bowl of the dip so they can spoon themselves what they want. Alternative: Serve the berries alongside individual ramekins of the dip. Then each eater has his own designated supply.

This dip also makes an excellent 2-minute dressing for a fruit salad, as well as a super topping for other fruit desserts.

2 pints strawberries
16-ounce tub nonfat sour cream
2 tablespoons sugar

2 tablespoons orange liqueur (or fresh orange juice)

Wash the strawberries and arrange on small dessert plates.

Whirl the sour cream, sugar and liqueur (or juice) in a blender. Mound the dip near the strawberries.

Serves 6.

Melon de Menthe

After a heavy meal, remember this addictive refresher. White crème de menthe is easy to find, inexpensive and can be used as a lively marinade for almost any fruit dessert.

1 cantaloupe
2 tablespoons *white* crème de menthe (or dash of mint extract in 2 tablespoons water)

Fresh mint leaves

Cut the melon in half and dispose of the seeds. Scoop out melon balls using a spoon or a melon baller. Add the white crème de menthe or the mint extract and water. Mix well but gently. Place in stemmed glasses or small dessert dishes. Refrigerate the melon until serving time. Top with fresh mint. Visually, the mint leaves make this dish. Use any left-over mint leaves in tea.

Serves 4.

Quick Fruit Hash

Fruit hash! A new concept. The word *hash* comes from the French word *hacher*, "to chop up," and yes, that is where the word *hatchet* comes from. So take your ax in hand and get chopping on some bananas.

This dish is light, pretty and quick. Pick up the main ingredients in one swoop of the produce section. Mix and match according to what's in season, knowing that bananas are always available to act as a base.

(Continued)

Served with hot popovers, this compote also makes a lively breakfast for guests. Set the guests to work on the nuts and fruits while you mix up the popovers. See the easy popover recipe on page 122.

See the easy popover recipe on page 122.

1/4 cup slivered almonds

2 bananas

1 pint strawberries

1 cup green seedless grapes

1/4 cup fresh orange juice (or orange liqueur)

Arrange the almonds in a single layer on a flat microwavable dish. Toast them in the microwave for 3 minutes or until they begin to brown.

Wash, hull and slice the strawberries. Wash the grapes and strip them from their branches. Peel and slice the bananas. Combine the fruit and juice in a bowl, tossing gently to mix. Distribute the fruit hash among four pretty dessert dishes or stemmed glasses. Top with toasted almonds.

Stovetop alternative

Same as above except sauté the nuts in a heavy pan over medium-high heat until they are fragrant and lightly toasted.

Serves 4.

Mango-and-Coconut Cup

Here's a quick fruit cup with a tropical air. This one is a nice relief after a heavy dinner.

2 14-ounce ripe mangoes, peeled and chunked

1/4 cup sweetened, shredded coconut

1 tablespoon fresh lime juice

1 tablespoon honey

Place all ingredients in a bowl and mix.

Serves 4.

Banana-and-Macadamia-Nut Stir-Fry

This warm fruit dish is fast. The bananas are browned and fragrant. Whole macadamia nuts add a crunch of luxury. Throw in a splash of rum or amaretto. If you prefer, use a dash of rum extract or almond extract in 2 teaspoons of water.

Consider this dessert when there's nothing in the house but a bunch of bananas or when you are too tired to do more than take a quick pass at dessert. (This dish can be made without the nuts.)

It's also a great snack when the next meal seems a distant dream.

2 firm bananas **2 teaspoons butter (or oil)**
¹/₄ cup whole macadamia nuts **2 teaspoons rum (or amaretto)**

Heat the butter or oil with the rum or amaretto over medium-high heat until melted and bubbling. Add the nuts and the bananas, sliced into rounds. Brown, turn gently, then brown some more. Just a few minutes will do it. Remove from the heat before the bananas turn mushy.

Serves 2.

Five-Minute Chocolate-Orange Mousse

Quick to make and with just 4 ingredients, this mousse is a good do-ahead dessert. Liqueur is one ingredient, but if you prefer to go nonalcoholic, use a dash of orange extract added to 2 tablespoons water.

³/₄ cup chocolate chips
12-ounce can nonfat evaporated milk
1 teaspoon unflavored gelatin

2 tablespoons orange-flavored liqueur

Garnish
Grated orange peel

This recipe can be made up to 1 day ahead.

Melt the chocolate chips in the microwave, using a microwavable container such as a Pyrex measuring cup. Cook the chips 45 seconds, stir and then cook them 15–20 seconds more.

Next, put ¹/₂ cup of the milk into a 2-quart saucepan and sprinkle the milk with gelatin. Use just 1 *teaspoon* of gelatin, not the whole little individual package. Let the mixture stand 1 minute to soften up the gelatin. Then stir over very low heat until the gelatin melts. Remove from heat. Add the remaining milk and the melted chocolate to the pan. Add the liqueur or extract mixture. Then whirl the whole works in a blender or food processor.

Pour into small bowls or into porcelain ramekins. Cover and chill in the refrigerator at least a few hours. Garnish with grated orange peel. Present this dessert with a crisp cookie or an orange slice on the side.

Stovetop alternative
Same as above except melt the chocolate in a double boiler or in a heavy pan over very low heat.

Serves 6.

Microwaved Bread Pudding

This is the impatient person's bread pudding. Ready in minutes, it's lighter than oven-baked bread pudding.

Presoaking the raisins in sherry or rum improves the flavor, but you can soak the raisins in water rather than alcohol. I make this with oatmeal bread, crusts and all. More delicate people may wish to remove the crusts and use a lighter bread.

1/4 cup raisins

1/2 cup sherry (or rum)

3 cups cubed bread, either stale or lightly toasted

4 tablespoons butter (or margarine)

2 tablespoons sugar

3 egg yolks

1 cup milk

2 teaspoons vanilla extract

Soak the raisins in the sherry or rum for 10 minutes.

If the bread is not dry and stale, toast it lightly. Then place the cubes in a microwavable cooking/serving dish. Set aside.

Next, in a small microwavable cup, heat the butter. Drizzle half the butter over the bread. Stir.

In a bowl, beat together the sugar, egg yolks, milk and vanilla. Add remaining butter and the *drained* raisins to the milk mixture. (Discard the raisin-soaking liquid.) Pour the milk/raisin mixture over the bread. Mix all together.

Microwave uncovered for 3 minutes, or until the eggs are cooked.

Walnuts and whipped cream on top would be nice, but just plain milk or cream is fine.

Serves 4.

White Chocolate Chip Cookies

These cookies are so popular that I triple the recipe, bake one-third and freeze the rest rolled into two cylinders of raw dough for later slicing and baking. Leftover cookies make an addictive crumbled topping for ice cream, puddings and baked fruits. This cookie travels well and is a good finale for a picnic or tailgate party.

Picnicking people seem to think that because they are eating outside, the regular laws of nutrition are suspended and they can eat all the cookies they want. In fact, each modestly sized cookie has only 4 grams of total fat, so one or two will not do you in.

1 cup ($^1/_2$ pound) soft butter
$1^1/_2$ cups sugar
2 teaspoons baking soda
1 egg

1 cup plus 2 tablespoons flour
2 cups quick-cook rolled oats
1 cup white chocolate chips

Heat the oven to 350°.

Beat the butter, sugar and baking soda until creamy. Beat in the egg. Gradually add flour and oats. Mix in the white chocolate chips. (This last move may have to be done by hand if your electric mixer balks at the heavy dough.)

Drop by mounded teaspoonfuls on a well-buttered baking sheet. Bake until light golden—about 10–12 minutes. Let cool until the cookies are firm enough to transfer to airtight storage.

Recipes always say to cool baked goods on a wire rack, but you can put the hot cookie sheets over your cooktops. Most will work nicely as cooling racks.

Store in a tightly covered container.

Makes about 5 dozen.

Blond Bomber Brownies

These brownies are not brown but cream-colored. Made with white chocolate chips, they are classically rich.

¹/₂ cup butter	**¹/₄ teaspoon salt**
3 cups white chocolate chips	**1 teaspoon vanilla extract**
2 eggs	**1 cup flour**
¹/₂ cup sugar	**¹/₂ cup walnut pieces (optional)**

Heat the oven to 325°.

Coat an 8" square baking pan with nonstick spray. Using a 4-cup measure or equivalent container, melt the butter and ²/₃ cup of the white chocolate chips by cooking about 2 minutes in the microwave.

The chips may still have some form and look unmelted. Just take them out of the microwave and stir to mix and melt. If not entirely melted after stirring, cook 10–20 seconds more.

Then, using an electric mixer and a large bowl, beat the eggs, sugar and salt about 5 minutes. Switch to low speed and blend in the melted butter/chips and vanilla. Add the flour and beat just until mixed. Stir in the remaining chips and the optional nuts.

Spread into a baking pan. Bake 35 minutes, or until done. Cool, then cut. Freezes well.

Stovetop directions
Same as above except melt the butter and chips in the top of a double boiler.

Serves 6–8.

One-Pan, No-Bowl Chocolate Cake

This recipe once achieved cult status because it is sublimely easy, very good and leaves few dishes in its wake. Named Jiffy Cake, Wacky Cake or Cockeyed Cake, depending on where one lived, the recipe has all but disappeared from the folk-cooking circuit. Now it's time to present this simple wonder to a new generation of home cooks. As with many recipes that sweep the country, the creator is anonymous. Let us toast this primitive guerrilla with cold milk as we down our warm chocolate cake.

Extra points for this cake: no butter, no eggs.

1½ cups flour	**5 tablespoons cooking oil (not olive oil)**
3 tablespoons cocoa	**1 tablespoon white vinegar**
1 teaspoon baking soda	**1 teaspoon vanilla**
1 cup sugar	**1 cup cold water**
½ teaspoon salt	

Heat the oven to 350°.

Grease a 9" square cake pan. Put the flour, cocoa, soda, sugar and salt right into the pan. Stir until mixed.

Now comes the really weird part. Make three little holes in the dry ingredients and pour the oil in one, the vinegar in the second and the vanilla in the third. Pour precisely 8 ounces of cold water over the whole thing. Don't lose faith, but stir the ingredients until mixed, until you can't see the white of the flour.

Bake for 30 minutes.

To dress up this cake, sprinkle a little powdered sugar on top. If you have a lace paper doily similar to the kind bakeries stick under their cakes, put the doily on top of the cake and sift the powdered sugar through it. This makes an elegant pattern and is a jiffy, no-cook topping for a jiffy cake. Kitchen-supply stores now carry plastic stencils for decorating cake tops with powdered sugar.

If you prefer more than a dusting of sugar, the Instant Chocolate Dip/Frosting in this chapter makes a good frosting for this cake.

Serves 6 as a main dessert, 8 if served as an accessory alongside a bowl of fresh raspberries or a baked pear.

Shameless Hussy Carrot-Spice Cake

There was a time when married women did not often work outside the home. They were called "housewives" (hous'wivz'). They were asked to make cakes for school bake sales and potluck suppers. The unspoken rule was that these cakes were to be made from scratch. Only a shameless hussy would try to pass off a cake mix as the real thing.

Here's how I did it:

1 box spice cake mix, made according to directions

1 cup grated carrots
¼ cup raisins

Heat the oven to the temperature suggested on the cake mix box.

Mix up the batter the way the box says, adding the carrots and raisins after the batter has been beaten. (Note that cake mixes now come with low-cholesterol directions.) Bake according to package directions. The baking might take a few minutes longer because of the extra ingredients. When the sides of the cake pull away from the pan, it's probably done.

If you bake the batter in a big single layer, it is easier to serve. Just sift powdered sugar on the cake and forget the frosting. (Layer cake, on the other hand, calls for butter frosting, but why go to all that work?)

The raisins can be used straight from the box or soaked in sherry or rum, drained and then added to the batter.   (*Continued*)

Serves 8.

Chocolate Variation

Whip up a chocolate cake mix, adding 1 cup grated zucchini and ¼ cup chopped walnuts.

Serves 8.

These two cakes will get you through the potluck/bake-sale stage of life.

Quick Chocolate-Chip Cake

This from-scratch cake is for those of you who want to bake a delicious but fairly healthy cake yourself. (See recipes above if you prefer to use cake mixes.) This is moist, good and quick—no butter or egg yolks. Chocolate-chip lovers can double the chip amount to 1 cup. Dieters can leave them out entirely.

2½ cups shredded fresh zucchini	**¼ cup unsweetened cocoa**
1 cup applesauce	**2½ cups flour**
1½ cups sugar	**1 teaspoon baking powder**
4 egg whites	**1 teaspoon baking soda**
1 teaspoon vanilla	**1 teaspoon cinnamon**
½ cup buttermilk	**½ cup chocolate chips**

Heat the oven to 325°.

Coat a 9" x 13" pan with nonstick cooking spray.

Grate enough zucchini to make 2½ cups. Use the large-hole side of the grater. Set aside.

In a large bowl, mix the applesauce and sugar together. Add the egg whites, vanilla, buttermilk and the dry ingredients. Mix. Add the zucchini. Mix and then pour in the cake pan. Sprinkle with the chocolate chips.

Bake for 45–50 minutes, or until the sides of the cake pull away from the pan.

Like all chocolate cakes, this is best served with cold milk.

Serves 8.

Apple Pie with Phyllo

This is a new, fast way to cook apple "pie." There's no crust to make or roll out, no peeling or coring of apples, no waiting an hour for the pie to bake. It's a special dessert that's delicious and only about 200 calories a slice.

The spiced apple filling is jet-cooked in the microwave, then topped with an easy crust made of store-bought phyllo (filo) pastry dough. It then bakes for just 12 minutes in the oven. The results? A pie full of fragrant spiced apples topped with a golden brown crust.

No microwave? No problem. Stovetop directions are given below.

The Filling
6 medium Granny Smith apples
$^1/_4$ cup frozen apple juice concentrate
$^1/_4$ cup light brown sugar
$^1/_4$ cup sugar
2 tablespoons flour
2 tablespoons fresh lemon juice
$^1/_2$ teaspoon ground cinnamon

$^1/_4$ teaspoon *each* ground ginger and nutmeg

The Topping
5 sheets phyllo dough, *defrosted*
1 tablespoon melted butter
1 tablespoon sugar

First, find and follow the defrosting directions on the package of phyllo. When ready to cook, with your defrosted dough at the ready, heat the oven to 400°. Coat a pie plate with nonstick cooking spray.

When making the filling, don't bother to core or peel the apples. Merely hold the apple, stem side up, on a chopping board and slice off appropriately sized pieces. Put the pieces in a large microwavable bowl along with the other filling ingredients. (Hint: Defrost and liquefy the frozen apple juice concentrate in a measuring cup in the microwave to get the amount just right.)

(Continued)

Mix the filling ingredients well. Cover the bowl with plastic wrap and microwave for 8 minutes.

Remove the apple filling from the microwave and put the filling in the pie plate.

Stovetop directions for filling

Just simmer the ingredients, covered, on the stove for about 20 minutes. Stir occasionally.

Now for the topping: Unwrap the phyllo layers only as you need them, for the dough crumbles easily if it dries out. As you work, the dough may crack and look like a big mess, but don't worry. Just like life, all's well that ends well, even if it's messy in between. Remember: You cannot kill this crust.

Just peel off about five layers of the dough, one by one, and lay them over the apples, basting each layer with melted butter and a sprinkle of sugar. Don't worry if you pull off two layers instead of one, or if they break. Just cover the filling with pieces of butter-basted, sugared dough. You can even scatter a few pieces of broken dough over the top. They'll look like pastry petals when cooked.

Then put the pie in the oven for 12 minutes, or until golden brown.

Serves 6.

Lemon Meringue No-Pie

Why waste time making regular piecrust? It's the uncertain manipulation of butter and flour for the certain purpose of gaining weight. Instead, go with recipes such as this Lemon Meringue No-Pie that has the filling and topping, but not the crust. Serve it either in a pie plate or in a fluted soufflé dish.

The Filling
1 cup sugar
$1/4$ cup cornstarch
$1^1/_2$ cups cold water
3 egg yolks, beaten
Grated peel of 1 lemon

$1/4$ cup lemon juice
1 tablespoon butter (or margarine)

The Meringue
3 egg whites
$1/3$ cup sugar

Heat the oven to 350°.

In a pan with a heavy bottom, combine the sugar and cornstarch. Add the water gradually, stirring until smooth. Stir in the beaten egg yolks. (Be sure and do these things off the heat.)

Now put this mixture on medium heat, bring to a boil, and boil 1 minute, stirring constantly. Remove promptly from the heat.

Add lemon rind, lemon juice and butter. Mix.

Pour into a pie plate or a soufflé dish coated with nonstick spray.

For the meringue, beat the egg whites until stiff. Gradually add the sugar.

Spread the meringue over the filling, making nice peaks here and there. Bake for about 15 minutes, or until it begins to turn golden.

Serves 6–8.

Shortcut Fruit Cobbler

There's a fast way to make fruit cobbler in the microwave. This one is made with blueberries and fresh nectarines or peaches, but you can suit yourself—all blueberries, all peaches or all nectarines. Just keep the amount of fruit steady at about 4 cups.

The Filling
- 2 cups blueberries
- 2 cups peaches or nectarines, stoned and diced
- 1 teaspoon cinnamon
- 1½ tablespoons cornstarch
- ¼ cup sugar

The Topping
- 1 cup low-fat biscuit mix
- ⅓ cup water
- ⅓ cup low-fat granola (or vanilla cookie crumbles)
- ¼ teaspoon cinnamon

Oil or spray a microwavable pie pan (or baking pan). Mix the fruits, cinnamon, cornstarch and sugar together gently. Place in the pie pan and cook uncovered about 8 or 9 minutes in the microwave, or until the mixture thickens. Stir halfway through the cooking time and again at the end.

Meanwhile, to make the topping, stir the water into the biscuit mix. Then take the hot fruit "pie" out of the microwave and clean up the spatters on the sides of the pan. Drop the dough by heaping teaspoonfuls on the cooked fruit until the surface is dotted with cobbles. (This is why this dish is named "cobbler"—because the dough looks like cobblestones. In Middle English, "cob" means "lump.")

Top each cobble with the granola and cinnamon. Don't omit them, because they give color, texture and extra taste to the dish.

Microwave the cobbler for 3–3½ minutes. Top with cream or whipped cream if desired.

Serves 4.

Sweet Brie Bake

Oh, here's to a warm and bubbling cheese topped with sweet apricot spread and pecans! This dish gets high marks for ease of preparation and visual appeal.

Serve the cheese hot on the coffee table after dinner. All guests pitch in and spread the warm cheese on cold slices of fruit. Fire and ice. A wicked combo. Crisp new apples are a fine choice, but cold ripe pears will get a standing ovation.

A big round of bubbling Brie can make a grand entrance at a larger party. Just increase the fruit-spread topping, nuts and oven time accordingly. Arrange several wedges into a faux round if you can't buy an entire round. No one will notice because the wedges all melt together in the oven. But here's the smaller version to start:

1 wedge Brie cheese (about 1/2 pound)   **1/4 cup pecans**
1/4 cup apricot jam (or all-fruit spread)   **4 cold ripe sliced pears (or apples)**

Heat the oven to 350°.

You don't have to cut the rind from the Brie, but do peel off the product label.

Put the cheese in a small baking dish with sides high enough to hold back the melting cheese. (If you can, choose a dish about the same size as the cheese, so the cheese won't spread out and melt all over like a Salvador Dali painting.)

Top the cheese with the jam. Sprinkle the pecans on top. Bake 7–10 minutes, or until warm and bubbling.

This dish is sensational right out of the oven.

Note
Warm Brie buried in preserves is sometimes served as an appetizer, but it is a far, far better thing to save its sweet richness for dessert.

Serves 4.

Three Cheese Ideas

Some recipes are so short and simple that they should be called ideas and not recipes. Here are some easy ways to serve cheese European style (after dinner) or, going more freestyle, as a snack or even lunch.

Brie Idea

Consider the delicious combination of a Brie slice, toasted walnuts and cinnamon. Here's how to make it as a dessert or snack for one. Multiply as appropriate.

First, on a small plate, toast 1 tablespoon of walnut pieces in the microwave for 1½ minutes. Take the plate out of the microwave. Put one slice of Brie on the same plate. Then transfer the nuts to the top of the cheese, shake on a sprinkle of cinnamon and run it again in the microwave for just 10 seconds. Served on crisp thin sesame crackers, this is fantastic.

Ricotta Ideas

Ricotta is a sweet fresh cheese. I think of it as cottage cheese that went to heaven. Mix some ricotta with a little liqueur and then top with a few nuts. Consider amaretto ricotta topped with almonds, or Grand Marnier ricotta with thin peeled orange slices plus a sprinkle of coconut.

Another idea: Mix chocolate chips into the ricotta, perhaps along with chopped pieces of dried apricot. Any tidbits of fruit, dried or fresh, are good with ricotta.

Still another thing to try: Ricotta can be made into a puddinglike dessert by running it in a blender with sugar or honey until smooth. Try 8 ounces of nonfat ricotta with 2–3 tablespoons of sweetener.

Gorgonzola Idea

Think of ripe pears or figs with a hunk of Gorgonzola on the side as a spread for the sliced fruit. Add pistachio nuts to the plate, and you will have happy munchers.

Layered Ice-Cream Cake

A do-ahead party dessert, this frozen mold features ice cream or frozen yogurt layered with cake or cookies, sweet sauce and tasty bits such as nuts, berries or granola. It is a spectacular finale and can be used as a birthday cake or as a holiday dessert. You don't cook this, but merely assemble the ingredients, putting them into a mold, layer by layer.

See below for ideas about ingredient combinations. The order and the ingredient amounts in this dish are not crucial, but you might follow these directions the first time through.

3/4 cup tasty bits (low-fat granola, nuts or berries)

8-ounce bottle nonfat dessert sauce (chocolate or caramel)

2 quarts compatibly flavored nonfat frozen yogurt (or ice cream)

1 frozen pound cake cut into thin slices, (or cake or cookies from list on p. 114)

Make this dessert at least 6 hours ahead.

First, watch the frozen yogurts melt on the counter. You can run a carton of frozen yogurt in the microwave for 20 seconds if you're in a big hurry. This makes new guerrilla cooks nervous, but it works reliably to soften the hard edges.

When the frozen yogurt spreads easily, take a 3-quart mold and put 1/2 cup of the topping (granola, nuts or berries) in the bottom, reserving the rest as a garnish. Next put in a layer of dessert sauce. Then add a layer of frozen yogurt, a layer of the second frozen yogurt and a thin layer of cake which you have cut into slices.

Keep going, putting down layer over contrasting layer—frozen yogurts, cake, sauce—until the goods run out or are almost to the top of the mold. (*Continued*)

Cover the finished dessert with plastic wrap or foil. Store in the freezer until party time. When ready to serve, dip the bottom and sides of the mold quickly into warm water and unmold on a plate, chilled if possible. Wipe up any little meltings on the serving plate with a paper towel.

Serve garnished with the reserved topping.

Finally, remember that this is *the* dish if you don't have time to cook a party dessert. It makes a spectacular ending without even turning the oven on.

It's also good instead of cake for birthday parties. Use a mold with a hole in the middle, and you have a place to put a big birthday candle.

Some good flavor combos are:

FROZEN YOGURT/ICE CREAM	SAUCE	BITS	CAKE/COOKIES
Vanilla/chocolate fudge	chocolate	walnuts	pound
Mint/chocolate	chocolate	chocolate chips	chocolate
Coffee/jamoca almond fudge	caramel	almonds	shortbread
Lemon/raspberry ices	berry jam	berries	ladyfingers
Pumpkin/butter brickle	caramel	walnuts	vanilla wafers

Other bits that can be added are white chocolate chips and coconut.

Serves 12–20, depending on how you slice it.

Lemon Ice Ring with Berries

Here is a light version of an ice cream mold. It's an easy lemon sorbet ring surrounded with fresh blueberries. It's also good with raspberries. This makes a pretty do-ahead company dish.

2 pints lemon sorbet
4 cups fresh blueberries (or raspberries)

2 tablespoons sugar

Let the sorbet soften at room temperature or run 20 seconds in the microwave. Put the softened sorbet into a ring mold that holds 5–6 cups. Freeze at least a few hours until firm.

Wash the berries. Mix in the sugar. Cut back on the sugar if the berries are very sweet. Store the berries covered in the refrigerator.

At serving time, unmold the ring onto a chilled serving dish. To unmold, put the ring quickly in hot water, turn upside down onto the serving platter, and shake loose.

Scatter the berries inside the ice ring and on top. Slice and serve.

This dish is excellent made with chocolate sorbet and raspberries.

Serves 6–8.

Frozen Peaches with Yogurt

Remember this recipe when you want a dessert kind of snack.

16-ounce bag sliced *frozen* peaches
1 cup nonfat vanilla yogurt

2 tablespoons powdered sugar
1 teaspoon vanilla extract

Run the frozen peaches in a blender or food processer. Add the remaining ingredients. Blend again, stopping to scrape down the sides if needed. Eat right away.

If you can't eat this dessert promptly, you can put the peaches in microwavable dessert dishes and freeze them briefly. Then run the dishes in the microwave for 1 or 2 minutes on defrost or low or until appropriately softened.

Serves 3–4.

Cheating Chocolate Sauce

¹/₂ cup nonfat chocolate frozen yogurt

Bless your little cheatin' heart. You whipped up a quick sauce just by taking some nonfat frozen chocolate yogurt and running it in the microwave. One-half cup of frozen yogurt should melt charmingly in 20 seconds, leaving a few still-cold, creamy presences in the middle. If you love running a spoon of ice cream in and out of your mouth the way you were told not to, you will like this "sauce." If you want more sauce, use more frozen yogurt and zap in 5-second increments until you get the absolutely perfect melt.

Serves 2.

Instant Chocolate Dip/Frosting

It's funny that we use dips before dinner as appetizers, but not after dinner as desserts. Here you can dip to your heart's content. Satisfy a chocolate attack with this simple microwaved sauce into which you may plunge whole strawberries, pear slices, ladyfingers or your fingers. What you'll need:

¹/₂ cup chocolate chips   **¹/₂ cup nonfat sour cream**

Run ingredients in the microwave for 1 minute. The dish will come out of the oven still black-and-white, a two-colored curiosity. Just stir for a few seconds into a smooth and glossy sauce that is one color: chocolate. If you refrigerate the finished dip, it will harden; but 30 seconds in the microwave will get it table-ready again.

The dip can also double as a frosting. It will cover the single-layer chocolate cake in this chapter. Refrigerate leftovers.

Serves 4 as a sauce.

1, 2, 3 Berry Sauce

1 pint basket blueberries (or other fresh fruit)

2 tablespoons sugar

3 minutes in the microwave

Blackberries or raspberries are good for this chunky sauce, but I like fresh blueberries best. Blueberry sauce over peaches or nectarines is another reason to love summer and another way to keep the kids quiet for ten minutes.

The only way you can goof with this recipe is to use too-small a bowl. Sugar bubbles up in a microwave, so cook this sauce in a big 2-quart bowl.

Put the berries in the big bowl, sprinkle with 2 tablespoons of sugar, wrap with microwave plastic and micro-cook the berries for 3 minutes. Serve on fruit, pancakes or ice cream. Remember the recipe as 1, 2, 3—1 basket of berries, 2 tablespoons of sugar, 3 minutes of cooking.

Serves 4 as a sauce.

Refuse to Cook

How to Avoid Culinary Slavery

Exactly *what* you don't cook and *when* you don't cook is your choice. You can declare that you never cook on weekends, or that you never cook breakfast—it's every egg for itself. You can even do what my friend Caroline does. She declares she never cooks at all—anywhere, anytime—and she pretty much sticks to it. As others may choose not to play golf or bridge, Caroline chooses not to play stove. Microwave, maybe. She'll associate briefly with microwavable frozen food, but hardly ever with a pot or pan.

To help you get started not cooking, learn this brief excuse:

Say that you are a victim of Food Affective Disorder, or FAD. When faced with a meal to be cooked, victims of FAD become depressed beyond the reach of Prozac. The only remedy is to sit daily under the bright lights of a restaurant.

Now, if you have never not cooked before, the first time out may be hard. All those starving children and significant others pouting and moaning. But they soon learn to pitch in themselves. Cook or starve—it's a marvelous motivator.

So where to start not cooking? The first-time guerrilla should consider not serving dessert. It's the easiest thing to not cook because everybody wants to look thin. Perhaps you should just read this chapter on desserts and call it a day. Don't lift a spoon or a chocolate chip. Then, at the beginning of the next meal where dessert might reasonably be expected, announce that there is bad news and good news. The bad news is that there is no dessert. The good news is that the dessert you're not going to have is certainly low-fat.

5 Spécialités de Your Maison:
Food to Make Your Reputation

FINDING YOUR HOUSE SPECIALTY

Finding Your House Speciality

In this chapter, you can get in touch with your inner chef by adopting some show-off recipes. As you use the ideas here, you may remedy the wounds sustained in the past, those psychic injuries caused by fallen soufflés, burnt toast and recipes that would not work. This chapter will make your inner chef free, joyous and whole.

Okay, maybe not. But we will have fun and find something good to eat. Specifically, this chapter offers a selection of recipes based on the home cook's need to produce reliable comfort food and dependable basics with a new twist. Please try on at least one recipe to see whether it fits as your house specialty.

With this chapter in hand, you won't have to write to your mother to get her heirloom recipes. Even if you are the world's worst cook, your culinary confidence can be raised here to at least the low intermediate level. And while bad meals do indeed happen to good people, we can lower those nasty odds. First, though, we need to look at how and why your culinary self-esteem may have been wounded.

Who Killed Your Cooking Confidence?

Many people have no self-confidence when it comes to their own cooking. They go out to dinner and then compare their food to the meals executed by professional cooks. Or else home cooks look at photographs of pinup meals—the centerfolds in food magazines—and think they should be turning out the same impossibly beautiful stuff in their own kitchens. These comparisons can lead to severe cooking dysfunction—people imagining that life is a soufflé and everybody but them can get it up.

This view of the food world is not true. You *can* produce good food at home without a degree from the Culinary Institute of America—good food that you can make over and over again just because you love the results.

So don't put yourself down if you can't whip up a Grand Marnier soufflé. Remember that most of us, most of the time, yearn for good mashed potatoes, not the fancy stuff. (Please see the recipe on page 138 for Guerrilla Mashed Potatoes.)

Finally, as you remember Aunt Helen's chocolate cake or Grandma's strawberry jam, so someone may remember at least one of the dishes you cook from this chapter. Nostalgia for old-time home cooking—it's part of the American dream.

No-Fail, No-Fuss Popovers

More of my family and friends have incorporated this recipe into their lives than any other in the book.

As you may know, popovers are tall custardy, muffinesque delectables, puffed with air and eaten warm right out of the oven. They may be slathered with jam, honey or any spread of choice. Though everybody who tastes a popover loves it, people don't cook popovers because they fear a popover flop or think that popovers require lots of butter.

But this recipe is easy, reliable and requires no butter. It has never failed me. It has become a favorite, a fixture, a reliable comforting treat. Here are the virtues of this recipe: It takes under 5 minutes to prepare in one large bowl, does not require a preheated oven, does not require the changing of temperature midstream like other popover recipes and does not require greasing the pan with gobs of butter. It takes 30 minutes to bake while you do other things. The batter can even be made the day before.

2 cups milk (skim is fine)
2 cups flour
4 eggs

$^1/_2$ teaspoon salt
1 teaspoon sugar

Don't preheat the oven.

Instead, put the milk in a large bowl. Add the flour to the milk. Add the remaining ingredients and beat until just mixed. Don't worry about a few lumps. Spray or oil two 6-cup muffin tins or popover pans and fill each cup two-thirds full. (Both kinds of pans come in nonstick versions, but spray even the nonstick pans so that the popovers won't tear when pulled out of the pan.)

Put the batter-loaded pans in the oven, which you will now turn to 400°. Leave the door closed. *Don't peek.* Bake about 30 minutes.

Take out. Eat. Acknowledge applause.

A great Sunday brunch dish, this is good served with juice, a fruit compote and a hot beverage. While the popovers bake, slice and dice the fruit, start the coffee, set the table, make the fire and read the paper.

If the popovers are done before the eaters show at the table, keep the popovers warm in the turned-off oven with the door ajar.

Makes 12 large popovers, which should serve 6. It also works fine if halved.

There are two secrets to baking. First, follow instructions exactly. This is no time for improvisation, especially when it comes to the correct proportions of flour, liquids and leavening agents. Second (and most neglected), make sure your oven temperature is accurate. Check it with an oven thermometer. Off-temperatures may be the cause of any past baking dilemmas. If the temp is not quite accurate, either get your oven fixed or adjust your temperature choice upward or downward to compensate.

Classic Crepes

The preceding popover batter makes enough crepe batter for 16 pancakes. For thinner crepes, add a little milk—about $1/4$–$1/2$ cup.

For each crepe, pour a small ladle of batter into a medium-hot nonstick skillet and cook briefly on both sides until lightly browned. (You can use a bit of butter in the pan if you like.)

Serve the crepes with syrup and fruits. Warm the syrup *briefly* in a ceramic dish in the the microwave. (Try 10 seconds to start.) For a topping, use nonfat yogurt and berries with warm syrup drizzled over all.

Crepes can be frozen. Separate the rounds with waxed paper and wrap in foil or plastic freezer wrap.

Serves 8.

Making Two Meals with One Recipe

For weekend breakfasts, serve both popovers *and* crepes with just one turn at the mixing bowl. Here's how to do it:

On Saturday, make the batter outlined in the preceding recipe for popovers. Use half the mixture to make a pan of 6 popovers. Save the other half in the refrigerator for Sunday, and use it to make elegantly thin crepes.

This double ploy will save time as it builds your culinary reputation. It's the answer to breakfast for weekend guests. Popovers on Saturday, crepes for Sunday brunch.

Serves 3. For 6 people, double the recipe.

One-Eyed Eggs

This recipe will make your rep with the younger set, but adults like it, too. Served as breakfast, a snack or supper, this dish has an almost-folkloric quality. It's known by wonderful names: Toad in a Hole or One-Eyed Jack. Basically, this is just one egg cooked in the center of a piece of bread. It's simple, easy and probably better for you than a three-egg omelet. Here's how to do it:

1 slice bread, toasted
¹/₂ teaspoon oil or butter
1 egg

Salt and pepper
1 slice Canadian bacon (optional)

Throw a piece of bread in the toaster with the setting on "Light." Get out the nonstick skillet, toss in the oil or butter and warm over medium heat. Take the lightly toasted bread and, using a round cookie cutter or a small glass, cut out a circle from the middle of the bread. You will now have in hand a piece of light toast with a hole in it.

Now throw the toast in the skillet, drop an egg in the hole, salt and pepper to taste and let cook for a minute or two. Then turn the whole thing carefully with a spatula and cook until the egg is done as much as you like. Don't worry if you break the yolk. The dish will still taste good.

Bacon variation

A piece of Canadian bacon fits nicely in the hole in the toast. Throw the bacon on the egg before you turn the egg over. Also, cook the cutout bread round in the skillet while this is all going on, and you will have a great big breakfast crouton to serve on the side.

These directions are for a single serving. Multiply as you wish.

House Salads

I used to futz around with salad, making my own mixes of three or four lettuces, including unusual homegrown varieties. Much was wasted. Ironically, because I was making such a big deal of the process—several lettuces, vinegars from obscure Italian hill towns, virgin oils—I didn't make salad often enough. There were many days when it was just too much trouble to get out the lettuce whirler and give the leaves their requisite ride on the lettuce merry-go-round.

Though store-bought baby-lettuce mixes and packaged greens were an obvious answer, I used to avoid them because they were expensive. Then I actually tracked the costs, counting what was wasted when I bought too much or forgot to harvest my own. Bottom line: It cost about the same no matter what.

Now I use the store-bought salad mixes and never look back at the years spent whole-heading. There's a salad every day because there's a salad uniform: one basic salad for summer, with a winter-holiday variation. Variety comes from the rest of the meal.

Here's the recipe for a simple salad with simple dressing. People ask all the time for my dressing recipe. They think I'm kidding when I tell them how easy it is.

Simple Salad with Simple Dressing

Greens (one handful)　　　　**Salt (two shakes)**
Olive oil (one drizzle)

Take 1 handful of baby lettuce mix or 1 handful of the other prepared lettuces. Throw onto a salad plate. Drizzle fresh olive oil over it. Shake two shakes of salt.

Notice: no salad bowl, no exotic vinegars, no tossing, no premixed dressing, no spices, no peeling of garlic, no garlicky rubbing of salad bowls, no salad bowl to clean, no wondering what bottle of dressing to pull from the back of the refrigerator.

Here are two quality-control tips for making this recipe work well at your house:

➡ The olive oil should be fresh, not marginally middle-aged. Buy a small bottle (which won't have the time to go stale) and store it in a cupboard away from the light. Don't be seduced by those big bargain cans of oil. Months from now, your dressings will taste of stale oil.

➡ The lettuce should be perky from the minute you see it to the minute you eat it. No brown edges or tired stuff. Lettuce mix can stay alert a few days if it is enclosed tightly in a plastic bag and put in the refrigerator as soon as it comes in the door. Treat lettuce just like milk: Keep it cold, or it will go off quickly.

Use quality ingredients, treat them well and you'll get quality results.

This recipe is for one serving. Multiply as appropriate.

The Winter Salad Variation

This is Son of the Simple Salad and very easy. It looks mildly spectacular around Christmastime and the New Year because the base of the salad is a star-shaped arrangement of endive.

Endive is not cheap, but a little goes a long way. If you can't find endive, use the small inner leaves of romaine lettuce.

Estimate a handful of lettuce mix for each serving.

The Salad	The Dressing
1 head endive	**Olive oil**
Salad greens (baby lettuce)	**Salt**

(Continued)

Peel off the endive leaves and arrange 5 leaves (or 3 leaves, if there are more people than endive) in a star shape on each flat salad plate. Place a handful of baby lettuce in the middle of the endive star. Drizzle with olive oil and give a shake of salt.

Use one of the optional toppings if you wish.

Optional Toppings

➡ Walnuts, slices of ripe pears, Roquefort cheese crumbles

➡ Pecans, thin slices of orange, bits of blue cheese

➡ Homemade croutons

Serves 6.

Shallot Dressing

This pleases people who like a little pizzazz in their dressings.

1 heaping tablespoon chopped shallots
1/2 cup olive oil
1 tablespoon balsamic vinegar
1 teaspoon Dijon mustard

1 teaspoon fresh tarragon (or 1/2 teaspoon dried herb)
Pinch of sugar
Salt and freshly ground pepper

Beat the ingredients together in a bowl.

Best if made ahead of time and allowed to mellow. Good on romaine lettuce with croutons.

Serves 6.

Lemon Dressing

So many people have commented on this dressing that I felt it had to make an appearance here. It is lighter and more delicate than the one above. Use this on those little baby lettuces.

1 teaspoon lemon zest, grated

3 tablespoons fresh lemon juice

2 cloves garlic, minced

$2/3$ cup olive oil

1 teaspoon freshly ground black pepper

$1/2$ teaspoon salt

Beat all the ingredients together.

Serves 8.

Toasted Baguettes

For a change, try this instead of the usual buttered garlic bread. Broiled bread is very guerrilla because it is a lot faster than baked garlic bread. But because it broils *fast*, don't leave broiler watch.

1 baguette
$^1/_2$ cup green onions, chopped

$^1/_2$ cup low-fat mayonnaise
$^1/_2$ cup grated Parmesan cheese

Heat the broiler.

Cut the bread in half horizontally, just as you'd do for garlic bread. Put the two pieces dough side up on a baking sheet and toast under a hot broiler about 2 minutes, or until lightly browned. Leave the oven door ajar so you can watch the process and prevent burning.

Chop the green onions and mix with the mayonnaise and cheese. Spread this mixture on the toasted bread. Stick back under the hot broiler for about 1 minute, or until the topping is lightly browned. Serve on a cutting board and let people cut the portion they want.

Serves 4–6.

Smoked Salmon-and-Pea Pasta

This is the easiest and most appreciated company pasta that I know. The green, pink and white color combination looks especially appetizing.

1 pound fettuccine	**4 green onions, minced**
3-ounce package smoked salmon	**1 tablespoon vodka (optional)**
10-ounce package frozen peas	**Salt and lemon pepper to taste**
2 tablespoons olive oil	**Parmesan cheese, grated**

Put the pasta pot on to boil. Cook the fettuccine according to package directions.

Mince the green onions. Dice the salmon. In a nonstick pan, cook the onions in the olive oil for 2 minutes over medium-high heat. Add the peas and vodka to the onions and cook another 2 minutes. Add the salmon, salt and lemon pepper. Stir gently to mix and heat just until warm. Don't overcook.

Drain the pasta. Put it in a serving bowl. Add the salmon/pea mixture. Pass the Parmesan. Add a green salad and French bread.

Serves 4.

Broccoli and Rigatoni

This is how to get broccoli into a veggie-phobe.

1 pound rigatoni	1/2 teaspoon salt
2 tablespoons olive oil	1/8 teaspoon red cayenne pepper
1 tablespoon butter (or margarine)	1 cup grated Parmesan cheese
3 cloves garlic, minced	
1 pound fresh or frozen broccoli (cut into bite-sized pieces)	

Put the pasta pot on to boil. Rigatoni will take about 10–12 minutes to cook after the water boils.

Put the olive oil and butter in a large frying pan. Add the garlic and sauté over low heat about 2 minutes. Be careful not to burn it. Add the broccoli, salt and cayenne. Stir-fry for another 5 or 6 minutes, or until done. Turn off to wait for the pasta to finish boiling.

Drain the pasta. Add to the broccoli. Scatter grated Parmesan over all.

Serves 4.

Peas 'n Pipes

Jack, the self-taught gourmet of my extended family, is a preschooler with graduate-school taste buds. He recently introduced me to a meal he named Peas 'n' Pipes, a dish destined to become the house pasta for short people who like to play with their peas and eat with their fingers.

The peas used are not the tiny petits pois, but the hefty ones toddlers can pick up easily. The pipes are hollow tubular pasta such as mostaccioli, ziti or rigatoni.

8 ounces hollow, tubular pasta	10-ounce package regular peas, frozen

Put on the pasta pot. When the water is at a full gallop, add the pasta and cook according to package directions.

While the pasta is boiling, stove-cook or microwave the peas, also according to package directions, or maybe even a little less, just to keep their color and plumpness. Season the way your little people like.

Present this dish in bowls, with the peas spooned over the pasta. Do not be surprised if the eater tries to stuff the hollow pipes with the peas. This is precooking behavior and is very auspicious. The young person might become a good cook and serve you when you have turned old and gray.

Serves 4 small ones.

"Rice" Pasta

This pasta side dish is a sneaky way to get the look of rice but the taste of pasta. It's faster than conventional rice.

When shopping, look in the pasta section for riso, a faux "rice" made of small well-behaved grains that fork up neatly into the waiting mouth. Because the shape is unusual for a pasta and the taste surprises people, it's a nice choice when you would like to do something different. Consider this as your signature starch.

Riso is especially useful for proper dinners when you want the taste of pasta but don't want to slurp spaghetti strings. Other small, polite pastas are called orzo, semi di melone (melon seeds) and acini di pepe (pepper kernels). Any of them will add luster to your pasta life.

1 pound riso

Like any good sidekick accompaniment, this is simple. It just needs to be cooked the way the package says and then seasoned the way *you* say. It's your choice, but a little olive oil and a bit of salt are all that's needed. Finely chopped fresh parsley would add color, but only if you have the time.

Serves 6–8.

Polenta and Turkey Sausage

To find the best American cooking, just sniff around your neighborhood. Here's the house casserole of Jana, the cook next door:

The Polenta Base
3 cups skim milk

1 tablespoon butter

¹/₂ teaspoon salt

1 cup yellow cornmeal

¹/₄ cup Parmesan cheese, grated

Mix the milk, butter and salt together in a heavy-bottomed saucepan. Heat just to the boiling point. Then turn the heat to low and slowly add the cornmeal to the milk, stirring constantly. Keep on stirring until the mixture gets thick and leaves the sides of the saucepan. There will be pops and glugs from the cooking cornmeal, but this is normal. Don't put your face right over the pot, or you may get spattered.

When done, mix in the Parmesan cheese and spread the polenta/cheese mixture immediately into a buttered or sprayed 2¹/₂-quart casserole. Set aside while you prepare the turkey sausage and sauce below:

The Protein and Sauce
³/₄ pound low-fat turkey sausage

¹/₄ cup Parmesan cheese, grated

1¹/₂ cups favorite store-bought spaghetti sauce

¹/₂ pound nonfat mozzarella cheese, shredded

Heat the oven to 325°.

Slice the turkey sausage into rounds. In a nonstick skillet, sauté the turkey over medium heat until browned, about 10 minutes.

Sprinkle the Parmesan over the polenta in the casserole. Add the sausage. Cover with the tomato sauce. Layer on the mozzarella. Bake until bubbling, about 30 minutes.

Let the casserole sit and settle out of the oven about 10 minutes while you make a salad to go with it.

Serves 4–5.

Adam's Rib
(Prime Roast Beef for Two)

This is an innovative way to roast a large prime rib and two baked potatoes while you do something more interesting than cook.

1 beef prime rib, 2–2¹/₂ pounds   **Salt, pepper, butter to taste**
2 large baking potatoes, scrubbed and
   pricked

At least the day before the love fest, go to a good butcher shop and have them cut a rib from a standing rib roast. The rib should weigh about 2 or 2¹/₂ pounds. They may try and sell you an 8-ounce rib steak, but hold out for a big slab of prime rib.

When you get home, cut off the excess fat around the edges of the meat. Then wrap the rib in foil and stick it in the freezer until it's a solid block. Don't cheat on the freezing part. Leave the rib in at least overnight.

Then, an hour and a half before you want to eat, take the frozen rib and stand it upright, bone side down, in a foil-lined baking pan with a washed baking potato on each side, the end of each potato pointing toward you. (The two potatoes act as bookends, holding up the rib.) Prick the potatoes in several places with a knife tip.

Remember: *Don't defrost the meat first.*

Set the oven to 400°. Place the meat and potatoes in the oven. It will take about 1¹/₂ hours to roast the beef medium rare. You can use an instant-read meat thermometer to make sure the roast has reached at least 160° before you take it out. Well-done roast beef will take longer—about 1³/₄ hours. *(Continued)*

When cooked, season the beef and potatoes to taste with salt, pepper, butter—whatever. (Remember salsa as a baked-potato topping if you're butter-aversive.)

Add a huge salad.

Serves 2 with leftovers.

Baked Steak
(A Guy Dinner)

One of the truths of culinary life is that you can bring a man to tofu, but you can't make him eat. Instead, try this hefty baked steak. It could not be easier. While it has a barbecue flavor and is smothered in sweetly browned onions, there's no barbecue fire to babysit, no turning of the meat or tight timing. In other words, stick the steak in the oven and go enjoy yourself.

Put in two russet potatoes to bake along with the steak. Then, at serving time, pour the cooked onions and barbecue sauce over the potatoes, too. (This is definitely guy cuisine.)

If you start preparation in the morning and let the steak marinate all day, the steak will have more flavor and greater tenderness.

1 sirloin steak, 2³/₄–3 pounds, about 2¹/₂" thick
1 cup dry red wine

18-ounce bottle favorite barbecue sauce
2 large onions, thinly sliced

Cut all the fat from the sides of the meat. Prepare a foil-lined baking pan with sides high enough to hold in the sauce/marinade.

Pour the wine and the entire contents of a bottle of your favorite barbecue sauce into the pan. Stir the wine and the sauce together in the pan. Add the steak. Turn the steak over a few times in this mixture to make sure that it's covered with the sauce.

Put the sliced onions over the steak. Spoon some sauce over them so they'll caramelize in the oven. (To caramelize means to get all sweetly brown.)

Cover the dish and refrigerate. For health's sake, don't taste the sauce after the raw meat has been marinating in it. Wait until the sauce has been cooked thoroughly in the oven.

An hour before dinner, turn the oven on to 425° and bake for 60 minutes until medium-rare, or until done to your taste. Slice the steak thinly on the bias (not straight up and down, but at a slant). Serve with the onions, potatoes and a salad.

This steak is bigger than what the 2 of you will eat for dinner, but the guerrilla cook likes to get a few meals out of just one effort. Leftover steak is great sliced and sautéed as an entrée the next day. It also makes good steak sandwiches.

Romantic Meals for Women

Readers looking for a romantic meal to make for a female should think twice about the two recipes above. Both of them are world-class wallows through meat-and-potato country, which is not the first choice of most women. Instead, try the Smoked Salmon-and-Pea Pasta on page 236 or the Crispy Critter Chicken on page 19.

Guerrilla Mashed Potatoes

Here you finally have it: quick-strike mashed potatoes that don't have to be peeled, cut into chunks, boiled or drained. This recipe also saves washing a pot and a colander. These potatoes succumb so willingly to mashing with a fork that they don't have to be passed through a ricer or attacked with a masher. And, most importantly, they turn out wonderfully tasty, though they are not loaded with fat and have no cream at all.

The secret is simple: They are made with russet potatoes that bake while you do other things. When the potatoes are done, slit them open, scoop the insides into a bowl, mash, add milk and seasoning. That's it.

As for the fat content, baking potatoes have so much natural taste that they don't need to be doctored with cream and so forth. I use skim milk on these, and you'd never know it. The only thing you have to remember is to throw the potatoes in the oven 1–1¼ hours before you want to eat.

If you are making a bunch of potatoes at once, let them cook an extra 15–20 minutes, or until they are soft when squeezed.

For each person, use:

1 baking potato
1 teaspoon butter

A shake or two of salt
1 tablespoon skim milk

Scrub as many potatoes as you need. Pierce each several times with a fork and bake in a 400° oven for 1 hour. (Use no foil. Don't even bother with a dish.)

Take the potatoes out of the oven when they are soft. Use pot holders to protect your hands.

Cut the potatoes down the middle. Scoop out the insides into a bowl. Mash. Add the butter and salt. Mash some more. Add milk until you get the texture you love.

This recipe is for one. Multiply as necessary.

Guerrilla Baked Stuffed Potatoes

Yes, you could make conventional baked stuffed potatoes, which means you must be very careful not to pierce the skins as you take out the inside of the potato. But this is unnecessary and time-consuming food surgery. So here's how to get the taste of baked stuffed potatoes without actually stuffing the potatoes or even using the skins at all.

Just dump the finished mashed potato mass from the preceding recipe into a greased casserole. Top with grated cheese. Parmesan, Monterey Jack or cheddar would work. Bake at 450° for 5–8 minutes.

Faux French Fries

Everybody likes french fries, but nobody likes the grease or the work of frying. This thick-and-chunky version is done in the oven and baked with just a bit of oil.

2 baking potatoes   **Salt and pepper**
1¹/₂ tablespoons oil

Scrub the potatoes and cut each in half lengthwise, leaving the peel on. Then cut each of the halves into 5 or 6 wedges, also slicing lengthwise. You will produce some nice big french-fry shapes. Put the wedges in a bowl of cold water for 15 minutes while you do something else. These wedges can soak as long as overnight, so the timing is not critical.

When you're ready to cook, preheat the oven to 500°. Pull the potatoes out of the water bath and roll them around in paper towels to dry. Then tuck them in a large plastic bag with the oil and shake back and forth until all are lightly coated.

To cook your "french fries," coat a cookie sheet with a nonstick spray and arrange the potatoes in a single layer. (They won't get crisp all over if you pile them on top of each other.) Bake for 15 minutes or until crisp and brown, turning once halfway through. Season to taste with salt and pepper.

Serves 4 and very well, too.

Eggplant for People Who Hate Eggplant

I am a convert who once regarded eggplant as a suspicious vegetable. I thought this ominously purple plant was surely how the Medicis poisoned each other: eggplant juice mixed with henbane, newts' tongues and stuff like that.

But here's what converted me: an eggplant spread that can be used as an appetizer on crackers, as a savory side dish or over scrambled eggs. For lunch, I eat the leftovers rolled up in iceberg-lettuce leaves. Almost everybody who has tasted this eggplant dish wants the recipe.

1 large eggplant	$1^1/_2$ tablespoons olive oil
$^1/_2$ cup walnut bits	$^1/_4$ cup fresh parsley, minced
$^1/_2$ cup onions, chopped	1 tablespoon fresh lemon juice
1 clove garlic, minced	Salt and pepper to taste

With a knife, pierce the eggplant through the skin here and there and microwave for 9–10 minutes, or until soft. The eggplant gets very hot, so use mitts when you pull it from the microwave.

Once the eggplant is out of the oven, you can slice it open to make it cool faster.

Now that the eggplant is cooked and cooling, just cook the chopped walnuts, chopped onions, minced garlic and olive oil together in the microwave for about $2^1/_2$ minutes.

Chop the fresh parsley.

When the eggplant is cool, pull and scrape all the meat out of the skin and chop it, too. (The meat pulls off most easily from top to bottom, going with the eggplant grain instead of against it.)

Put the chopped eggplant meat in a bowl. Add the other ingredients. Mix.

Do not omit the parsley. It gives freshness and needed color.

Time mellows and improves this dish, so it can be prepared as much as 2 days ahead. This is a great convenience when you want to serve it as an appetizer at a dinner party.

Makes about 2 cups.

Pesto Upper

In folk medicine, basil is regarded as an upper, Nature's gentle antidepressant. Long ago, pots of basil were used in church, presumably to keep people awake for the sermons. Even today, reputable books of herbal medicine suggest wearing a few drops of basil essential oil to increase mental alertness.

I have taken liberties with classic basil pesto, reducing the oil from the usual 1/4 cup to 2 tablespoons.

I've also speeded up the usual process. You don't have to pull each little leaf from every stem. Cut off only the big stems at the bottom of the bunch. Throw everything else that's fresh and green in the food processor or blender.

1 bunch fresh basil, big bottom stems removed (about 2 cups)

2 tablespoons olive oil

4 large cloves garlic

1/4 cup pine nuts (or walnuts)

1/4 cup grated Parmesan cheese

Salt and pepper to taste

Wash and dry the basil leaves, discarding any black leaves. You can whirl the basil dry in a lettuce whirler.

Put the oil and garlic in a food processor or blender. Whirl. Stop. Scrape down the sides if all is not blended. Whirl again. Then add the remaining ingredients and blend. Process until smooth. Scrape out the contents with a spatula. Cover tightly with plastic wrap that sits right on top of the pesto surface. Refrigerate. Can be frozen.

Makes about 1 cup, which goes a long way.

The flavor is so intense that just a touch will do in a recipe. See how many ways you can use basil pesto. Try a spoonful on pasta, in sandwiches, over vegetables, on eggs, in salad dressings and spreads. It's one thing I never have to throw out because by the end of a week, it's all used up. Don't worry if the top surface discolors a bit during storage. That's normal. Use it anyhow.

Healthy Corn-and-Cranberry Stuffing

Full of good vegetable bits, this hefty dressing has no butter at all. My relatives add butter at the table if they feel their butter rights have been violated.

3²/₃ cups chicken broth

2 garlic cloves, minced

1 bunch green onions, chopped

4 stalks celery, chopped

2 cups *dried* cranberries

14¹/₂-ounce can small white onions, drained

2 9-ounce cans whole corn with liquid

1 cup walnut pieces

2 12-ounce packages corn-bread stuffing mix

Salt, pepper and poultry seasoning to taste

Put the chicken broth and minced garlic into a big pasta pot. Bring to a boil. Throw in the green onions and celery. Let them simmer for 4 minutes, or just until beginning to soften. Remove from heat.

Add the cranberries, small white onions, corn bits (with liquid) and walnuts. Stir. Add the stuffing. Mix again gently.

Season to taste with salt, pepper and poultry seasoning. Some corn-bread stuffings are highly seasoned. Others need a flavor boost.

Stuff the bird just before baking. Bake the stuffed bird according to your usual recipe.

Refrigerate any extra stuffing and then bake it in an oiled casserole for the last 30 minutes of bird cooking. Cover with foil if you prefer a moist dressing.

Fills a 25-pound turkey. Halve the recipe for a 12-pound bird.

Spaghetti-and-Sausage Dressing

Spaghetti in a dressing? Come on!

Trust me on this one.

4 ounces spaghetti, broken in pieces

$^1/_2$ pound low-fat turkey sausage

3 ounces provolone cheese, grated or chopped

1 egg, beaten lightly

$^1/_2$ teaspoon Italian seasoning

Salt and pepper to taste

Put the pasta pot on to boil. Cook the spaghetti according to package directions. Drain.

Cut the sausage into bite-sized pieces and sauté in a large frying pan over medium heat until lightly browned.

Grate the cheese using the large holes on the grater. (Or chop the cheese finely.)

Add the drained pasta to the sausage. Add the remaining ingredients. Mix.

Just before you are ready to roast the bird, fill it with the spaghetti stuffing. Roast the stuffed bird according to your usual recipe.

Stuffs 1 roasting chicken. Double the recipe for a turkey.

Cranberry-and-Orange Salsa

When it comes time for cranberry sauce, here's an easy way to avoid the same old canned cylinder of cranberries. Make this up to 2 days ahead and store covered in the refrigerator.

The truth, though, is that some eaters will miss the canned cranberry sauce. You'll be safer serving both—homemade and canned.

2/3 cup pecans, toasted
2 cups dried cranberries

3/4 cup orange juice
1 tablespoon orange skin, grated

Put the pecans, single-layer, in a microwavable dish and micro-cook for 2 minutes or until toasted. (Or, you can toast them in a nonstick pan on the stovetop.)

Add the nuts to the remaining ingredients in a food processor or blender and puree until mixed. That's it.

Serves 6–8.

Guerrilla Tip

Shortcut: Put a can of whole cranberry relish in a serving bowl. Add grated orange peel and chopped pecans. Mix. Top with whole nuts and a few more gratings of orange peel. Clean up the sides of the bowl before serving.

Tofu with Peanut Butter

This is different, incredibly fast and should appeal to anyone who likes peanut butter or Thai food. Essentially, it is a chilled slab of tofu, covered in a peanut sauce, perked up by chopped green onions. This serves 2 and can be served on a bed of lettuce leaves. It's a nice dish for you and a friend on a hot day when nobody feels like cooking.

Don't knock this snack until you try it. It makes a nice summer lunch, too.

14-ounce piece tofu (medium texture, if possible)
4 tablespoons chunky peanut butter (reduced-fat works fine)

Garnish
2 to 4 green onions, finely chopped
chopped peanuts

Take the chilled slab of tofu from the package and drain. Slice in half horizontally. Put one piece on each plate.

Put the peanut butter in a microwavable bowl. Cook 30 seconds in the microwave or until it spreads easily. Divide the peanut butter, spreading half on each slice of tofu. Scatter the chopped green onions over each piece, using 1 or 2 onions a person depending on personal taste. If you feel fancy, throw chopped peanuts on top.

Serves 2.

Quick Sugar Icing

Part of the pain of making a cake is having to think of an icing. Here's a cake icing that takes about 90 seconds to make. It can be made plain (just powdered sugar and milk) or fancy (with flavored extract). There's no butter to soften, to cream or to migrate to your hips.

1 cup powdered sugar
2 tablespoons milk

Optional
2 drops flavored extract (mint, rum or almond)

In a microwavable bowl, mix the powdered sugar, milk and optional flavoring. Micro-cook for 15 seconds. Drizzle the icing over the top of the cooled baked object. Let the baked object sit uneaten at least until the icing sets.

Ices 1 layer. Double the recipe for a big layer cake.

Don't Compare Yourself to a Chef

Why Doesn't My Food Look Like the Stuff in Restaurants?

Answer: It shouldn't.

Comparing your home cooking to a chef's is not only a case of apples and oranges, it's apples and oxen. You and a chef are not at all alike. Here's why:

First, chefs choose to cook. However, it's not *your* profession. And though retailers would like you to believe that home chefs are just a waffle iron away from being great cooks, the natural discrepancy between your home cooking and a chef's has more to do with who is getting paid to focus on what. If you made the money Julia Child makes, you'd be a lot more excited about your Thanksgiving turkey.

Second, chefs don't have to peel, slice and chop the food for cooking. They have kitchen help for that. No wonder chefs promote from-scratch cooking in their cookbooks: Someone else does the scratching. Do you think the chefs on TV do the peeling and chopping for all the little dishes of ingredients? They don't. Next time the credits roll at the end of a TV cooking show, notice how many people are on the kitchen crew.

Third, chefs often don't have to go shopping for their food. Many ingredients are delivered right to their kitchen door. The chicken travels to them. You, on the other hand, have to drive to the supermarket to pick yours out of the lineup at the poultry counter.

Fourth, chefs don't do their own dishes. It's why their recipes are not focused on one-pot guerrilla cuisine and are not concerned with minimizing dish mess. On TV, chefs just stick the dirty dishes under the counter. I try that, but they're still there the next day.

Fifth, chefs don't have kids in the kitchen, pulling the pots and pans out of the cupboard and onto the floor.

But still, because of what we see in magazines, we continue to measure ourselves against those damnably beautiful pictures of food. But if you knew how these photos were made, how much fussing and visual lying go into them, you'd stop the comparisons.

Here's the truth: Professional food stylists are hired to make the magazine layouts look fabulous. Food stylists are paid to go to antique stores to get just the right tabletops, linens, dishes and silver. They visit modelmakers who sell acrylic ice cubes that won't melt under the photographer's lights. Food stylists paint food, stuff pies with potatoes for "crust lift" and spray everything in sight with olive oil for shine. Unless it is in an actual product-advertising shot, their ice cream is made of margarine, corn syrup and powdered sugar.

So stylists are food cosmetologists. They make the food sexy. But—this is the ironic part—their food is often inedible.

Why? Because the flame on the photogenic crepes was made with lighter fluid. And the reason the turkey looks so plump is that it is almost raw, but dyed to look cooked. And the "milk" in that wonderful bowl of cereal is white glue. That's so the flakes won't sink.

Now maybe you've burned a thing or two during your cooking life, and maybe not all your meals are wonderful; but never in the 50,000 estimated meals you have or will cook during your lifetime have you ever served cornflakes in white glue.

Surviving Your Own Hospitality

Eliminate the idea of a perfect meal from the host part of your cerebrum. You are a home cook with the attractive whiff of culinary innocence about you, not a professional chef with an ego on the line. Forget about trying to be an award-winning restaurant. Your guests want you, not a perfectly boned salmon. Better to schmooze with your friends and serve an imperfect meal than to banish them to the living room while you struggle mano a mano with dinner.

Laugh at all natural disasters connected with entertaining—the burning of rolls, the ice shortages, the misunderstanding between you and the recipe. Be honest. Admit to guests that the roast is charred beyond recognition or that the chicken will not be done until next Tuesday. Traditional face-saving advice says to disguise your culinary mistakes and/or pretend they didn't happen, but I say, save hypocrisy for when you really need it.

The next way to make your life easier is to whine for help. I have never met a guest who was not willing and even grateful to be asked to help. Guests pitching in can be fun. It gives them something to do besides thumb through the old magazines on the coffee table.

Many guests have show-off specialities they'd love to perform. Some may excel at salads, others at the barbecue grill. Even a culinary klutz can scrape a carrot or dice celery.

When guests ask what they can bring, never say, "Nothing." At least tell them that a bottle of wine would be a great help. For the complex meals at holiday clan-gatherings, ask stay-over relatives to bring the different courses. It takes forethought (or a spatial-relations expert) to arrange refrigeration for the dishes they may bring. Transporting and storing the food in insulated ice chests can solve this problem.

Next, plan ahead. You may be delightfully spontaneous, but save it for bed. For guest meals, organization is the key to fun. Write down the menus, the shopping list and the game plan of what you will cook when.

Always listen to the inner voice that tells you to cut back on overly ambitious menu plans. It is the voice of sanity. For instance, you may want to make just one or two of the recipes here—not the whole menu plan—and then supplement the meal with store-bought or deli items.

Whatever you plan, work ahead. As much as you can, prepare the food ahead of time so you can relax when people arrive. Many of the recipes in this section can be prepared ahead.

About overnight guests: Put them on their own for the minor meals. Breakfasts and lunches are ideal for solo cooking. Sometimes guests are relieved to be in charge of their own feeding.

In the evening, after dinner, indicate where the coffee, tea, juice, cereal, fruit, toast and jam are, so guests can get their own breakfast while you sleep. For lunch, buy bread and sandwich fixings, along with fruit and cookies, and show people where they are.

Indicate the approximate location of the dishwasher and tell them you don't mind how it's loaded.

And then don't mind.

Do-Ahead Supper

The centerpiece of this low-key Italian meal is——

Baked Pasta with Three Cheeses

This dish can be made a day ahead and stored covered in the refrigerator until baking time.

2 pounds penne (or another bite-sized pasta)

1 pound nonfat ricotta cheese

1 pound goat cheese

1/2 cup milk

8 sun-dried tomatoes, oil-packed, drained and chopped

Salt and pepper to taste

1/2 cup grated Parmesan cheese

1/2 cup seasoned bread crumbs

If you are going to cook this casserole as soon as it's assembled, heat the oven to 350°.

Set your large pasta pot to boil. When at a full boil, cook the penne for 2 minutes less than the package directions.

Butter or spray a 3-quart casserole. In a big bowl, mix the ricotta, goat cheese, milk, tomatoes, salt and pepper. Remember that the cheeses will have salt, so go easy.

Drain the cooked pasta and mix gently into the cheeses. Put the resulting pasta/cheese mixture into the casserole, top with the Parmesan cheese and bread crumbs. Baked uncovered for 40 minutes or until bubbling and beginning to brown.

Serves 6–8.

Green Salad

Mixed baby lettuces　　　　　　**Salt**
Olive oil　　　　　　　　　　　　**Curly endive (optional)**
Balsamic vinegar

Buy the already-mixed baby lettuce—one handful a person. Dress the salad simply with olive oil, balsamic vinegar and salt. (Safe proportions: 4 parts oil to 1 part vinegar.) If there's curly endive on the produce counter, add some to the mix. The tartness works well against the sweetness of the pasta-and-cheese casserole.

Peasant Tart with Apples

This do-ahead fresh-fruit tart can be assembled in less than 10 minutes. The look and smell of this dessert are appealingly rustic. One can imagine the country-style crust being kneaded by good sturdy hands.

Thank heavens, these hands are not yours, for you will be using frozen puff pastry, found on the dessert side of the supermarket freezer. It typically comes in a long rectangular package.

17$^{1}/_{4}$-ounce package frozen puff pastry　　　**1 tablespoon butter**

2 or 3 Granny Smith apples, cored,　　　　　　**2 tablespoons sugar**
peeled and thinly sliced　　　　　　　　　　　　**$^{1}/_{2}$ teaspoon cinnamon**

Take the pastry out of your freezer. Remove half the package. Rewrap the rest and return it to the freezer for your next tart. Leave the working half on the counter to defrost until it's pliable enough to handle without cracking. This should take about 15–20 minutes, but don't let the dough sit any longer.

Heat the oven to 450°.

Core, peel and thinly slice the apples. Butter or spray a pie pan or a fluted ceramic tart dish. Lay the unfolded dough across the dish. Crimp up the edges in a fluted pattern, using big, peasanty fingerprints. If the corners of the rectangular dough get too bulky for the round dish, just pull off some of the dough.

Arrange the apples in a pattern on top of the dough, and brush them with butter. Sprinkle with sugar and cinnamon.

Bake 10–12 minutes, or until brown on the edges. Make this before the guests come and, if you like, rewarm in a 200° oven. A dollop of vanilla ice cream or nonfat frozen yogurt is an excellent topper.

Serves 6–8.

An Elegant Offering

If you want to go fancy in the dinner department, try this meal for 4. It begins with a delicious vegetable spread that can be made ahead, the leftovers used later as a sandwich spread. Even people who hate vegetables like this.

The main course is easy roasted game hens lavished with green grapes, accompanied by grilled vegetables, couscous and a salad. The meal is finished with berries capped by white chocolate.

If you are in a hurry, but still crave the illusion of luxury, I've provided sneaky shortcut alternatives below.

Healthy Vegetable Pâté

This dish looks and tastes rich and creamy, but is mostly green beans and chopped eggs flavored with basil. It should be made with fresh basil, not the dried herb.

Many people avoid cooking with fresh green beans because they think you have to take the string off each bean and then lop off the two ends. In fact, the newer bean varieties are practically stringless, only the stem ends need to come off. If you hate the whole fresh-bean business but want to try this dish anyway, you can substitute frozen green beans. Make sure that you drain them well after cooking and that you cook them lightly so they're still green.

But here's how to do it with fresh beans:

1 pound green beans (stem ends trimmed)	**2 teaspoons lemon rind, grated**
1 tablespoon olive oil	**Light mayonnaise to moisten**
2 onions, chopped	**Salt and lemon pepper**
6 hard-boiled eggs	**Small toast rounds or crackers**
6 tablespoons fresh basil, finely chopped	

Set the eggs to boil. Simmer about 10–12 minutes. Cool, peel and halve.

Cut off the stem ends of the beans and steam or boil them until tender. Alternatively, a microwave takes about 7 minutes to steam a pound of beans covered in plastic wrap.

Sauté the onions in olive oil over medium-high heat on the stovetop until tender, or microwave them along with the olive oil for about 5 minutes, more or less, depending on how big the onions are. (Cover the onion/oil mixture with microwave plastic wrap.)

Cool the cooked foods until they are safe to handle.

In a food processor, mix the beans, onions, eggs, basil and lemon rind until they are coarsely chopped. You'll have to do a few batches. *Do not overprocess the ingredients.* Use the pulse technique (off, on, off, on) to keep from making mush.

Mix all the chopped food ingredients with light mayo to moisten, plus salt and lemon pepper. Put in a serving dish, garnish with basil leaves or lemon rind and surround with crackers or toast.

You can make this the day before a party and store it refrigerated and tightly wrapped.

Serves 6–8.

Shortcut
The jet-fast alternative to this recipe is simply to steam fresh green beans, marinate them in a vinaigrette dressing, drain and serve them as a finger food before dinner. Don't even bother to cut off the little stems: They serve as handles.

Roasted Game Hens with Grapes

Rock Cornish game hens are the cute company dinner. Almost everybody likes having a tiny bird all to himself. And when a grand platter of small golden birds appears on the table surrounded by clusters of green and/or red grapes, you and yours will be content.

Game hens are found in the frozen-bird section next to the ducklings. Defrost the birds in the refrigerator the day before cooking. Put a dish under them to catch the defrosting liquid.

About 2 hours before dinner, take them out of the refrigerator.

4 Rock Cornish game hens
1 lemon, thinly sliced
2 tablespoons honey

2 tablespoons cooking oil
Salt and lemon pepper
Grape clusters

Heat the oven to 350°.

Wash the birds inside and out and pat dry.

Place bits of sliced lemon inside each bird. Arrange the birds in a lightly oiled or sprayed baking dish. If you use foil lining for easy cleanup, make sure there's spray on the foil so the birds won't stick when you try to lift them onto the serving platter.

Combine the honey and oil. You can warm the mixture for a few seconds in the microwave to encourage their mixing; the warmth encourages them to mate. Dab this mixture over the birds, reserving some for a later baste.

Put the birds in the oven and set a timer for 30 minutes. At that time, baste with the honey and oil, this time scooping up the pan juices, too. Then cook another 30 minutes, basting again right before the finish. If the birds are getting too brown, tent with foil.

Total cooking time should be about 1–1¼ hours depending on the size of the birds. They are done when the legs go up and down freely, or when the temperature in the thigh is 180°. If there's any doubt, let them cook longer.

Serve surrounded by grape clusters. Scissors are helpful for cutting the big clusters into serving size.

Serves 4.

Grilled Vegetables

You don't have to light the outdoor grill for these, but can run them in the oven along with the game hens.

2 medium yellow squash	2 medium onions
2 medium zucchini	2 tablespoons olive oil
2 red bell peppers	Salt and pepper

Prepare the vegetables, cutting them into chunks. Lay them fetchingly in a baking dish. Brush with the oil. Season well with salt and pepper. Bake at 350° for 1 hour, or until they begin to brown. They are also good served at room temperature.

Serves 4.

Couscous

Couscous is an easy-to-make, fluffy grain dish. Prepare according to the package directions.

Serves 4.

Green Salad

Either raid your produce drawer for salad fixings or buy the baby-greens salad mix. Serve with olive oil and salt. Period.

Use 1 handful for each person.

Strawberries Dipped in White Chocolate

2 pints fresh, sweet strawberries   **1 box (6 squares) white chocolate baking squares**

Wash the strawberries and let them dry.

Microwave the chocolate, unwrapped and in a microwavable cup, for 2–3 minutes. Stir halfway through the cooking time. Take out of the microwave *even though the chocolate still has a shape and appears to be unmelted.* Stir until smooth.

Stovetop directions

Place the squares in a heavy saucepan, stirring over very low heat until melted.

Now, holding each strawberry by its green top, dip it about halfway into the melted chocolate. Then put the berry onto waxed paper for about 30 minutes or until the chocolate is firm.

These are best if not made too far ahead—a few hours before dinner is fine. Refrigerate. Serve with a crisp cookie.

Serves 4.

Shortcut: Berry Fondue

Melt the white chocolate as the dinner dishes are cleared. Then let your guests do the dipping and eating. Don't even wait for the chocolate to firm up. Eat it warm and call it berry fondue.

All the eaters can use the one central melting pot, but the healthy dipping rule is that each berry gets submerged only once.

Lex-Mex Supper

Oh, how many of us love Mexican food.

If it isn't too hot.

If it isn't too spicy.

If it doesn't stray too far off the beaten burrito path.

And so a softer, gentler kind of Mexican cuisine has evolved in the United States. Its general rule is this: The farther away from the Rio Grande, the fewer the hot peppers. Cynics have named this kind of cooking "Lex-Mex": Mexican food that would be accepted on New York's Lexington Avenue.

But, when it comes to cooking for guests whose taste you may not know, Lex-Mex cooking makes sense. It is safe cooking and, if done with regard for flavor, it is good. After all, you can always add the hot sauce, but you sure can't take it out.

Check out the hot-sauce offerings in the Mexican-food department of your supermarket. Today, Tabasco is just one of several alternatives.

The following menu is hefty. Steak, beans, tortillas, fresh corn—these will satisfy the heartiest eaters. This is what to serve your kids when they come home from college with members of the football team in tow.

Shrimp Salsa with Chips

I've done my own oven-baked chips and I've done store-bought, and store-bought are best.

1 large package tortilla chips
14-ounce tub fresh salsa

$1/2$ pound small shrimp (cooked)
2 tablespoons fresh cilantro, chopped

Put the chips in a basket lined with a pretty napkin.

(Continued)

Check the liquidity of your salsa before you add the other ingredients. If it's too juicy and likely to drip as a dip, drain out some of the juice before mixing.

Mix the remaining ingredients right in the serving bowl. Clean up the sides of the bowl with a towel. Garnish with cilantro leaves.

Serves 6.

Steak Fajitas

Tender steak rolled in a hot tortilla—that should hold them for the main course. A choice of toppings makes this a do-it-yourself kind of dish. The toppings can be made ahead.

The tortillas may also be wrapped ahead, ready to warm in the oven just before dinner. The steak is quickly fried at the last minute.

The way to eat this dish: Place some steak slices in a tortilla, add the toppings of choice, roll up and eat with your fingers.

Chilled Mexican beer improves this dinner for those of drinking age.

The Toppings
1 bunch green onions, finely chopped
3 fresh tomatoes, chopped
4-ounce can chopped green chili peppers
2 avocados, mashed and salted
1 teaspoon fresh lemon juice

The Wrappings
18 corn or flour tortillas, 6–8" diameter

The Steak
3 pounds beef fillet or top sirloin, thinly sliced
1/4 cup cooking oil
Salt and pepper to taste

Prepare the four toppings and put each in a small serving bowl. Cover and refrigerate.

Fresh lemon juice added to the mashed and salted avocado will discourage browning. Covering the avocado surface with plastic wrap also helps.

Separate the tortillas into two piles. Wrap each pile with foil. Set aside to warm later.

When about to eat, put the tortillas in a 400° oven for 15 minutes and no longer. Set a timer.

Heat the oil over medium-high in a large skillet. Add the sliced steak. Fry until sufficiently browned. Add salt and pepper.

Bring the steak and the hot tortillas to the table. (Take the foil off the tortillas and serve them wrapped in a cloth napkin.)

Place the steak slices on the tortilla. Add a bit of the various toppings. Roll and eat.

Serves 6 with abundance.

Black Beans and Red Peppers

The red peppers floating in the black beans look pretty. Altogether, an appetizing color combo.

2 15-ounce cans black beans, drained   **2 fresh red peppers, seeded and chunked**

Microwave the peppers 4 minutes covered in plastic wrap. Meanwhile, warm the beans in a serving pot on the stovetop. Scatter the red peppers over the black beans.

Serves 6–8.

Easy Corn

6 ears fresh corn

Bring a big pot of water to boil. Strip the corn of the husks and silk. When the water boils, throw in the shucked corn, clap on the pot top, turn off the heat and let sit, without taking off the cover, for 10–15 minutes. Serve with salt and/or butter.

You can also microwave corn in the husk, two or three ears at a time. Two ears take about 5 minutes. This is fine for one or two people, but when guests come, cook the corn all at once in the big pot of water.

Serves 6.

Chocolate Cinnamon Frozen Yogurt

Chocolate touched with cinnamon is a Mexican treat. This should be done hours ahead so the yogurt can refreeze solidly in the mold.

1 quart chocolate frozen yogurt
1 tablespoon ground cinnamon
1 fancy mold (or use a bowl that can go in the freezer)

Optional Garnish
Chocolate curls and a cinnamon stick

Bring a quart of chocolate frozen yogurt home and leave it on the kitchen counter to soften while you do other things. (Warming in the microwave for 20 seconds helps the process along.) When soft enough to stir, put it in a bowl and mix in the cinnamon.

Place the dessert in a fancy mold. Freeze. Unmold by dipping the sides briefly in hot water. If desired, garnish with chocolate curls and a cinnamon stick.

Note

To curl chocolate, take a square of semi-sweet baking chocolate and a vegetable peeler. Make believe that you are peeling skin from the sides of the chocolate square, over and over again. These peelings are known as "curls."

Serves 6.

The Traveling Box Supper

In general, kitchen guerrillas avoid occasions that entail ironing napkins. That means they find ways to entertain guests other than a stuffy, multi-course sit-down dinner.

Here's one sure way out of that sit-down dinner. It's called The Traveling Box Supper. Jettison the formalities and kidnap your friends to a park, beach or scenic spot. Load each one up with his or her own container of supper—it's a multi-course meal in a sack—while you take care of beverages for all. Even easier is pulling off a traveling supper in your own backyard, or even, on a rainy night, in picnic style on the living-room floor.

Grown-ups are delighted by the informal format. Kid guests are relieved that they don't have to sit still at a table. If, however, you're doing this at home, steer the children to a spot where it won't make a difference if they get food on the floor. I've done this party with four generations of family. They love it because everybody can drift around talking to everybody else. If you're having supper outside where there are no chairs, bring along folding chairs with backs for the comfort of the elders.

In this version of a traveling supper, each guest's feed bag will contain a Brie-and-beef sandwich, guerrilla dill pickles, whole tomatoes to be eaten out of hand, fast homemade lemon sugar cookies and pieces of seasonal fruit.

The easiest and prettiest containers to use are the gift-giving bags sold next to the paper gift wrap. Save the bags in which you receive gifts, or if it's a really special occasion, go out and buy gift bags and then line them with coordinated napkins before you place the food in them. Add extra paper napkins for mopping up chins.

This meal can be prepared entirely ahead, which is a great virtue to those of us who like to be guests at our own parties.

Serves 6 adults.

Brie-and-Beef Sandwiches

If you really want to go uptown here, you can pan-fry filet mignon to medium rare and use thin slices of that as an elegant sandwich filling.

Easier and cheaper, however, is thinly sliced roast beef from the deli.

6 very fresh French bread rolls (sour-dough or sweet)

1½ pounds roast beef, thinly sliced

1 pound ripe Brie, thinly sliced

2 tablespoons horseradish mustard (or other favorite mustard)

1 bunch watercress, heavy stems discarded

Spread the rolls with the mustard, both sides. Layer on the sliced beef and Brie. Top with watercress. Wrap tightly. Refrigerate until time to pack up and leave.

If cholesterol is a concern, omit the cheese and make sure that the beef is trimmed of all fat.

This sandwich is also delicious on rye bread.

Serves 6.

Guerrilla Dill Pickles

1 jar refrigerated kosher dill pickles

1 cucumber, sliced lengthwise and halved

If you like crisp new pickles, young and barely beyond the cucumber stage, you will love this idea. There is no cooking, just planning ahead. Here's how it works:

In the dairy case, find the refrigerated kosher dill pickles that describe themselves as "always crisp." Now take these pickles home and eat them. When the pickles are gone, keep the jarful of pickling liquid in the refrigerator while you locate a large cucumber.

You are now ready to make guerrilla pickles. Just slice up the cucumber into pickle-shaped sticks and put them in the jar full of pickle juice. Refrigerate, leaving at least overnight, making sure that the cucumbers are covered by the liquid. Turn the jar upside down to make sure the liquid reaches all the cucumber.

Don't use the juice more than once, and don't keep the second crop more than a week or so. They lose crispness.

Serves 6.

Tomatoes

6 to 12 ripe tomatoes   **Salt**

Just add 1 or 2 small ripe tomatoes (wrapped) to each bag. Also tuck away a small salt-shaker. (Most stores sell a miniature version of the round cardboard salt container.)

The accepted technique when I was a child was salt and bite and salt and bite, bending over to drip the juice on the ground rather than on oneself. Not very elegant, but really good on a hot summer's day.

Off-season, if the tomatoes in the store aren't looking very appetizing, substitute cherry tomatoes or Roma tomatoes.

Lemon Sugar Cookies

These cookies can be made up to a day ahead and are the fastest baked cookies I know. This recipe uses a biscuit mix, which now comes in a low-fat version. The surprise here is that you can use a biscuit mix to make cookies.

2 cups dry biscuit mix

$^2/_3$ cup sugar

$^1/_3$ cup milk

5 tablespoons vegetable oil

1 egg

1 teaspoon vanilla

Skin of 1 lemon, finely grated (optional)

Heat the oven to 350° and grease or spray a baking sheet.

Combine all ingredients, beating with a spoon until blended. This will not look like regular raw cookie dough, but don't worry. It works out. Drop by tablespoonfuls onto the baking sheet. Make three rows down the long way to give them room to spread.

Bake 8–10 minutes, or until the edges and bottoms get light brown. Do not wait for the tops to get brown. This is a *white* sugar cookie. Sprinkle lightly with sugar.

Makes about 15 cookies.

The Shore Dinner

This dinner offers a salad, a seafood stew and a good ice-cream dessert. Hot French bread is a must with this one.

Serve the salad first. Once guests get into the hands-on seafood stew, they won't bother with salad.

Green Salad with Feta-Stuffed Olives

The Salad
Salad greens, chilled
Vinaigrette salad dressing

The Topping
6-ounce can large whole black olives, pitted
6-ounce container feta cheese, flavored with basil and tomato
Olive oil (optional)

Serve a crisp green salad with a basic vinaigrette. Over the top, scatter black olives that have been stuffed with bits of feta cheese. This cheese now comes already flavored with basil and tomato, but you can use plain feta, too. Just push bits of the cheese into the pitted black olives. The bigger the olive, the easier the stuffing. A splash of olive oil over the stuffed olives gives them gloss. Refrigerate until ready to serve.

Note
Unpitted olives with strange-sounding names are all the rage, but have a little respect for the dental work of friends and don't add unpitted olives to salads.

Serves 6.

Fast Cioppino

This seafood stew can be made partly ahead. You can add the seafood at the last minute to simmer in the sauce.

The Sauce

1 tablespoon olive oil

1 medium onion, chopped

2 cups marinara sauce (or store-bought cioppino sauce)

2 8-ounce bottles clam juice

$1/4$ teaspoon ground pepper

Salt, if needed

In a large skillet over high heat, cook the onions in the olive oil until soft. Add the remaining ingredients. Bring to a boil and simmer over very low heat for 5 minutes.

If making this dish ahead, now is the time to cover and refrigerate.

The Seafood

16 small cherrystone clams, scrubbed (or 16 green-lipped mussels)

1 pound raw medium shrimp (shelled or not, your choice)

1 pound fresh snapper (or other firm local fish), cut in pieces

$1/2$ pound sea scallops, cut in half if very large

The seafood mix can be varied. This recipe includes shrimp, snapper, sea scallops and clams.

Ask guest to shell their own shrimp at the table, picking them right out of the chowder. This works well with the smaller shrimp that have insignificant veins; but if you want big shrimp or your guests aren't the kind to plunge into a chowder, buy cleaned-and-shelled shrimp.

Look for clams that are tightly closed. Don't use any that won't close.

Add the clams to the sauce bubbling in the large skillet. Cover and cook 5 minutes. Add the shrimp, fish and scallops. Cover and cook another 5 minutes, or until the clams open. Don't be alarmed if they take a while to open. Some clams don't give up easily.

Serve in soup bowls. Have warm French bread available for mopping up the juices. Cioppino is really good with cold beer or a hearty red wine. Place a big bowl in the middle of the table for discarded shells.

Serves 6.

Ice Cream with Chocolate Sauce and Coffee Beans

This deep, rich chocolate sauce will convert you into using your microwave for cooking. Five ingredients, five minutes. Try it.

The Sauce
4 ounces chocolate chips
1/4 cup strong coffee
1 tablespoon butter
2 tablespoons half-and-half

2 tablespoons rum (or amaretto or other favorite spirit)

Garnish
Chocolate-covered coffee beans

Put all the ingredients into a large measuring cup or bowl. Cover tightly with plastic wrap. Micro-cook for 4 1/2 minutes.

Use a pot holder to remove from the microwave and take off the wrap carefully. The sauce may not look finished—some chocolate bits may still look unmelted. Never mind. Just whisk the ingredients, and all will change before your eyes into a smooth, rich sauce.

This sauce can keep up to a week in the refrigerator, so you can make it ahead. Rewarm uncovered in the microwave for 1 minute.

The Ice Cream

There is now wonderful nonfat ice cream on the market. It feels and tastes like the real stuff. Buy a flavor that goes with the chocolate sauce. Or choose a nationally distributed chocolate sorbet that is dense with great flavor. Then you can have chocolate on chocolate.

Spoon the warm chocolate sauce over the ice cream. Top each serving with a chocolate-covered coffee bean.

Serves 6–8.

A Classic Comfort Meal

When it comes to cooking for weekend guests, the expectation is that the food must be fancy. Too bad. Guests often crave simple comfort food. Dishes like meat loaf are always welcome.

Meat Loaf Cynthia

1 pound lean hamburger

1/2 pound spicy bulk pork sausage

1 large grated carrot

1 cup cornflakes

1 egg

1 medium onion, finely minced

3 tablespoons fresh parsley, chopped

Salt and pepper

1/3 cup ketchup

Heat the oven to 350°.

Mix all the ingredients except the ketchup in one large bowl. Place the mixture in a meat-loaf pan, smoothing the surface. Bake for 50 minutes. Then top with ketchup and bake for 10 minutes more, or until done. Looks colorful with a sprinkling of freshly grated raw carrot down the middle of the tomato-red loaf.

Serves 6.

Cheating Vegetable Pasta

Here's a sneaky way I invented to cook both vegetables and pasta using just one pot.

1 large pot boiling water

1 pound rigatoni (or favorite pasta)

10-ounce package frozen peas

Seasonings

Salt, pepper, a dash of olive oil, Parmesan cheese

Bring the pot of water to a boil. Add the pasta of choice and cook according to package directions. Then, about 2 minutes before the pasta is done, dump in the peas and let them cook merrily with the pasta.

Drain the contents of the pot. Toss with salt, pepper and a bit of olive oil for gloss. A sprinkle of Parmesan cheese crowns this two-for-one dish.

Serves 6.

Salad with Roma-Tomato Chunks

Salad greens	**Olive oil**
Roma tomatoes, chunked	**Salt**
Croutons	

There are ways to get yourself all set up for easy salad making—see the Guerrilla Tip below—but if you don't feel like making salad from scratch, buy a prewashed, packaged lettuce mix.

Add a few red Roma tomatoes cut into chunks. Romas are the smaller oval-shaped plum tomatoes and are the secret of a tomato lover's survival during winter and spring, when hothouse cardboard varieties are the norm.

If you have access to good store-bought croutons, use them. Many bakeries now sell great croutons. Some salad mixes come with croutons. Taste for quality before you add them.

Splash olive oil and a few shakes of salt on the salad.

Guerrillas love do-ahead salad making. They can prepare a whole produce drawer full of greens to use all week long.

Here's how: Get several different kinds of greens and submerge them in water in a clean kitchen sink. Whirl the greens dry, batch by batch. Wrap in a large towel, put the towel of greens in a big plastic bag and then lay all that in the bottom produce drawer of your refrigerator. Leave the bag open at one end for a little ventilation. Now you are prepared for any event involving the ingestion of lettuce.

French Apple Charlotte

Here's another do-ahead dish, a dessert that can be prepared ahead and shoved in the hot oven as you sit down to dinner.

8 cups peeled, thinly sliced apples (Granny Smiths are good)
1/2 cup sugar
3 teaspoons apple pie spice
1/2 teaspoon grated lemon peel

Salt to taste
1 cup water
3 cups soft whole-wheat bread crumbs
3 tablespoons melted butter

Combine 6 cups of apples with the sugar, spice, lemon peel, salt, and water. (Reserve 2 cups of apples for the topping.) Set aside. Toss the bread crumbs with half the melted butter. Then spray a 2-quart casserole with nonstick spray. Put in one-third of the bread crumbs and then layer with half the apple mixture. Repeat, ending with bread crumbs. Arrange the remaining apple pieces in a pleasing pattern on the top. Drizzle with remaining melted butter.

Cover with foil (or the casserole's top, if it has one) and bake in a 350° oven about 45 minutes. Then uncover and bake about 15 minutes more, until the apples are tender and crumbs are crisp. Lovely topped with frozen nonfat vanilla yogurt. The yogurt melts into a sauce for the warm apples.

Alternatively, if you don't want to bake the dessert at the last minute, you can make French Apple Charlotte early in the day to serve at room temperature.

Serves 6–8.

The Small Cocktail Party

Come for drinks. That's the standard invitation, but the wise hostperson knows that guests will be grateful for plenty of food—not the prettied bits of fluffy cocktail stuff from chichi cookbooks, but food that can take the place of dinner. Many guests, in fact, count on having dinner at cocktail parties. It's dinner in little bits, but it works. It's the cocktail buffet.

The cocktail buffet is a way to keep the starving masses happy and full while they drink. It's also a way to repay dinner invitations without excessive pain. At the cocktail buffet, everybody gets to walk around and have fun—even the people giving it.

Hosts and hostesses, though, sometimes worry overmuch, particularly about the bar and the serving of drinks. But you do not have to stock up like a commercial bar. You do not have to know how to make the drinks they teach in bartender school. You do not have to hire a bartender. People would rather make their own mixed drinks, anyhow. They know just how they want them.

So you relax. Just have white wine chilled and opened with wineglasses at the ready. Then indicate to guests that other choices are available if white wine doesn't suit them.

Below is a basic list of what to have on hand to cover most requests. Change it to suit your own needs. Add to it as you can.

Chilled white wine (chardonnay/ sauvignon blanc)

Red wine (Beaujolais/cabernet)

Good chilled beer—an imported brew or a domestic designer beer

Vodka

Gin

Dry vermouth (for martinis)

Scotch

Bourbon

Sparkling soda water

Mineral waters

Tonic (quinine water)

Soft drinks

Juices

Lemons and limes

A bottle of white cocktail onions

Don't worry about having an array of different glasses. It's old-fashioned to be fussy. One hefty, good-looking stemmed glass can cover a lot of territory. I serve everything in rustic-looking stemmed glasses from Mexico. These glasses are large. Martini drinkers just love my glasses.

As for the food, which hostpeople worry about, too, trust the six recipes below. They will see you through a cocktail party for about 12 people. Most dishes can be made ahead or require only a bit of last-minute warming.

Ginger Nuts

These are a good do-ahead solution for cocktail nibbles.

1 egg white	$^1/_4$ cup sugar
1 teaspoon cold water	1 teaspoon grated fresh lemon peel
1 pound lightly salted mixed nuts	1 teaspoon grated fresh ginger

Heat the oven to 300°.

Beat the egg whites with the cold water until frothy. Add the nuts and stir. Combine the sugar, lemon peel and ginger. Pour them over the nuts and coat evenly.

Put the nuts on a single layer on a greased cookie sheet. Bake for 20 minutes. (Stir after 10 minutes of baking.) Cool. Stir once while cooling. Store in an airtight container. These nuts take 1 day to mellow to their best.

Makes 3 cups.

Lemony Hummus Dip

Surround this hearty bean dish with your favorite dipping vegetables.

15-ounce can garbanzo beans (drained and rinsed)

2 cloves fresh garlic, pressed

3 tablespoons fresh lemon juice

1/4 cup plain yogurt

1/4 teaspoon ground cumin

Salt and pepper to taste

Olive oil (optional)

Put all the ingredients except the optional olive oil in the blender. Cover and process, stopping to scrape down the sides so all the ingredients get mixed.

Serve spread out thinly on a dinner plate, with dipping vegetables at the ready. Drip a little olive oil on the top of the spread if you wish. It gives a nice taste and a fresh glisten to the dish.

Makes almost 2 cups. If the crowd is large, prepare two batches.

Crab Pizza

Crab dip meets pizza. This winner is easy and very popular with guests. There are two shortcuts in this recipe: a ready-to-heat pizza shell from the supermarket and ready-to-eat frozen crabmeat.

1/2 cup low-fat mayonnaise

1 teaspoon fresh lemon juice

1/4 teaspoon curry powder

6-ounce package frozen crabmeat, thawed and squeezed dry

1 cup Swiss cheese, shredded

Salt and pepper to taste

11" ready-to-heat pizza crust (such as Boboli)

1 tablespoon green onions, chopped

Combine the first 3 ingredients. Mix. Add the crabmeat, cheese, salt and pepper. Mix.

(Continued)

Advance preparation

Cover and refrigerate now if making ahead.

When ready to bake, heat the oven to 450°. Grease a cookie sheet. Spread the above mixture over the pizza. Top with the green onions. Bake about 10 minutes, or until topping is puffed and toasty. Cut into 12 wedges. Serve right away.

Serves 12. For a larger, hungrier party, make two pizzas.

Sausage Bites

The choice of sausages is now so dazzling that it's safe to say we are in The Era of Designer Sausages. Today's sausages are made with chicken, seafood and turkey as well as pork, beef, lamb and tofu. Each section of the country has its own favorites, but here are two general rules for choosing a sausage to serve in bite-sized bits at a cocktail party:

➡ Stay away from sausages that would normally be used at breakfast.

➡ Buy already-smoked sausages rather than fresh sausages or ones where bits of ingredients are stuffed loosely into a casing. The loose ones will crumble, which you don't want here. You need a sausage that will stay together when it is cut and speared.

As for flavors, look for chicken sausage made with a Santa Fe chili bite or for turkey sausage sparked up with sage. There are many others.

Sausages (sliced into bite-sized pieces)   Parsley (garnish)

Select a variety of your favorite smoked sausages. (Figure on 1 6" sausage per person. You can freeze leftovers.) Cut the sausages into bite-sized pieces and fry until warm.

Garnish with parsley.

Serve with toothpicks for spearing the bits. Provide a receptacle for the used toothpicks as well as plenty of paper napkins.

Don't worry if the sausages cool on the serving table. They will, but they're still good.

Warm Brie with Jalapeño Topping

This recipe gives a little bite to Brie cheese.

By cutting the Brie in half horizontally, you get two appetizers for the price of one. You can assemble this recipe ahead and cook it briefly in the microwave at the last minute. Jalapeño-pepper jelly may be found in large supermarkets in the jam-and-jelly section.

1-pound piece Brie
¹/₂ cup jalapeño-pepper jelly

¹/₂ cup toasted pecans, finely chopped
Crackers or bread rounds

Cut the cheese in half horizontally. (Leave on the rind. Take off the product label, if any.)

Place one of the halves, cut side up, on a microwavable plate. Spread half the jelly on the cheese. Sprinkle with half the nuts.

Microwave about 30 seconds, or until the cheese begins to melt. Serve with crackers. Repeat directions with remaining cheese, jelly and nuts.

I assemble both plates ahead, store them covered in the refrigerator, microwave one and when that's gone, microwave the other.

Serves 12.

Corn Mini-Muffins

These are pretty and a sure hit with guests. Bits of pimento-stuffed olives peek from the top of each little muffin.

10-ounce package corn-bread mix

24 pimento-stuffed green olives (3-ounce jar)

Heat the oven to 400°.

Coat a mini-muffin pan with nonstick spray. Make up the corn-muffin mix according to directions. (It may require an egg, milk or both.) Fill each muffin cup three-quarters full. Press an olive, pimento side up, into each cup. Leave the top third of the olive sticking out above the batter. Bake 13–15 minutes, or until done.

Makes 24 mini-muffins.

Setting the Stage for a Great Time

There's No Business . . .

Entertaining is show business. You're the producer/director. Guests are the audience, the menu is the script and your house is the stage. The next day, the reviews should read: "A good time was had by all." And that "all" should include you—the marvelous, ever-so-clever and talented hostperson.

Now, it's easier to dazzle the audience when the stage looks grand, the lighting spectacular and music bright and lively. And everybody—yes, even self-confessed imbecile hosts—can set a good stage. Here's how:

Start before your audience even gets to the door. Stage the front entrance dramatically. Thread a string of small, clear, outside lights on a tree. Downlight (or uplight) a plant outside. Scatter Mexican luminarias to light the sides of the walkway. Wire a pretty wreath to the apartment door. Collect metal food graters at garage sales and put a votive candle inside each. (The light flickers through the grater holes.) Gather pots of flowers near the front door. Hang flowerpots off the porch railings or from the outside wall next to the front door. Nurseries have all kinds of hanging devices for flowerpots. The point is to say "Welcome." And once you have one or more of these ideas

in place, you can keep using them over and over again.

I know one fine person, James The Kind and Good, who pins a handmade poster to the front door anytime guests are coming. The poster welcomes guests by name. Needless to say, James gives great parties because each guest walks in the door feeling valued and welcome.

As for self-adornment, I always figure it's more important to dress up the front door than to dress up the hostess. Well, okay, no sweats or torn jeans, and I do make sure that the hot rollers are out of my hair by the time the doorbell rings. When it comes to hosting costumes, a guerrilla wears anything that is clean and not lying on the floor of the closet.

Next, continue the stage setting inside. Turn the houselights down. Dimmers are a great mood-modifying tool, especially in the dining room. Place candles all over the stage—living room, dining room and kitchen, too. Try to vary the candles in height—high, low and in-between. Candles are great in a kitchen, especially tall dramatic ones on a stand. Nobody expects it. And a semidark, candlelit house means guests won't see the dust or the third-degree burns on the dinner rolls.

If there's a working fireplace, work it. If it's summertime, fill it with green ferns. If the fireplace is there but not working, fill it with candles.

Five-disc CD players are a host's delight. Keep the volume low enough so that people can hear each other. All generations and musical subgroups seem to like or at least tolerate Gershwin and Cole Porter. Light baroque music will do, too—Vivaldi and also the frothier classic offerings of Mozart. Almost everybody likes nostalgic pop music collections, starting in the 1940s and going up through the 1970s.

Scents are important, though they are often overlooked in entertaining. Rev up the pleasure index with potpourri and good room sprays. I soak a cotton ball in scented essential oil and tape it to the back of a picture frame that hangs near the front door. Lavender, rose, gardenia, and orange blossom are the universal favorite scents. Recent research says men find the scent of cinnamon buns sexually stimulating, but breakfast buns are difficult to work into a dinner menu.

As for the dining room table itself, the simplest centerpiece will do. You don't have to go to a florist to buy a clump of stiff carnations dyed weird colors. Better a few daisies and some low votive candles.

All the china doesn't have to match. Napkins either, though it is nice if they are in the same family—all country checks and stripes, or all contemporary.

Guerrilla Tip

Here's how to handle the pressing of cloth napkins with a guerrilla tactic: passive ironing. When the napkins come out of the drier, fold them and place a clean washed brick on top of them. The weight presses the cloth napkins very nicely. Two bricks should do for most households.

Carry out just some of the above ideas, and you will be the finest guerrilla hostperson on the block.

Guerrilla Recipes from Home

Many good grass-roots dishes are lost to the world because home cooks don't write down their recipes. Here's a place to record your own guerrilla recipes and ideas. Then your descendants will be able to make what Grandma (and Grandpa) made because they can find it here. Also, next year, when you get a bad case of recipe amnesia, you can look back and see exactly how you made that good dish that Eddie (or Carol) loved so much.

And yes, you can write in a book, no matter what your third-grade teacher told you.

Acknowledgments

It has always astonished me that people put personal ads in the newspaper to talk to their dead relatives: DAD, YOU WERE THE GREATEST. LOVE, TONY AND BETH. But here I am, about to thank a dead person in print, which shows you should never feel superior to anyone for anything, because you might end up doing the same thing yourself.

So, a tip of the hat to Jackie Gleason, wherever he is now. When I knew him, he was a Broadway comic, a musical-comedy star and the first adult to get me giggling about food. When I was a little girl, I had many a midnight dinner with him and my father, his show's producer.

My dad thought it perfectly reasonable to keep a child up past midnight. So, of course, did I. I went out partying with the guys and watched what Gleason did with food. He found new uses for the holes in the middle of black olives, used his napkin as a hat and murdered manners just to amuse a little girl. I loved it and ever since then, I've been on the alert to the comic possibilities of food.

Thank you, Jackie Gleason. I hope they give you the message.

I have many others to thank. Nancy McKeon, food editor of the *Washington Post*, who got me off and running on this book with her encouraging letter. Carolyn Snyder of the *San Jose Mercury News* was the first editor at a major daily to take me on as a columnist. I thank them and Michael Bauer at the *San Francisco Chronicle*, who offered support by being the first to pick up my column, "Guerrilla Entertaining." I am also one of many helped by Adair Lara at the *Chronicle*.

Thanks also to Lorraine Gengo, who got me into the column business in the first place. Also much appreciated are Maria Carmicino and Paul Eberhard of King Features Syndicate, who called one day and asked if I would like to be King-featured. Wendy Marcus, my editor at King, has been a wonderful audience. I also thank Ted Hannah, Richard Heimlich, Phyllis Pitruzzello and the King Syndicate sales force. Jeff O'Connell deserves thanks, too, for helping me understand the legal issues behind the writing.

A special acknowledgment to my family who ate the food, read the text and provided opinions, ideas and recipes: Doug, Teri, Jack and Sydney Hessel, Stephen Hessel, Susan Burgess, Logan Hessel, Geoff Hessel, who did much fine eating over the years, and Lucy and Nicola Hartman who also pitched in. Our Queen Mother, Lucy II, added her valuable two cents, as did Susan and John DeRoche.

Then I'd like to salute those friends who offered their palates and stomachs as test sites for these recipes. If the recipes have been tested carefully (and they have), and if you grow to love and use them, thank the following folks, all of whom offered praise, hoots, new ideas or their own recipes:

A chief co-conspirator was Joan Zischke, mother of eleven mouths, who invented her own form of guerrilla cooking and shared it with me. Warm appreciation to Cynthia Regier and her family. They were a beta test site. Others who inspired were Chez Panissians Tom McNary and Mimi LeCocq, who let me watch in their kitchen for four years, taking what I wanted for my own unorthodox culinary purposes. Margaret Smith, she who headed entertaining at *Sunset Magazine*, was an early encourager.

Thanks also to Eleanor Battafarano, Helen and Ed Bigelow, Tom Blakeslee, Blanche Brownell, John and Jana Davids, Larry and James Dawson, George Foy, Callie Gregory, Maia Hansen, Bea Hessel, Jennifer Hopkins, Elaine Kamian, Maribeth Malone, Robin Simmons, Mac Small, Nancy and John Snyder, Marion Stegner, Don Stunkard, Katherine Wessel and Carolyn and Gil Wesson.

A thank you to Carol Field, who put me in touch with a great agent, Fred Hill. And thanks to Fred Hill for introducing me to my perspicacious editor, Bob Wyatt, who masterminds Wyatt Books for St. Martin's Press.

Thanks to Peg Bracken and M. F. K. Fisher for being my heroines.

Last, my gratitude goes to Gene Antisdel who got me my first writing job. He has been after me for twenty-five years with this simple mantra:

"Make words."

Index